Our Gift to You

Thank you for purchasing this book and supporting the work of the Prosperity Economics Movement, which is creating meaningful alternatives to the myths, costs, guesswork, and risks of "typical" financial planning. As our thank-you, we're giving you a FREE 30-page playbook:

*The 12 Principles of the
Prosperity Economics Movement*

It will help you gain Inspiration and Education, and it includes a journal for Activation of each Principle.

Get your free copy at ProsperityEconomics.org.

Additionally if you'd like "Permission to Spend: How To Spend Your Principle, Save a Fortune on Taxes, Increase Your Cash Flow… and Never Run Out of Money!" the QR code below will access it, or you can go to ProsperityEconomics.org/permission.

Additional books by Kim Butler

(All are in formats for readers, listeners, and Kindle fans.)

Your Guide to Activating Prosperity (Kim's story; only available at www.ProsperityThinkers.com/action)

Busting the Financial Planning Lies (the first book written, a story about two options with your finances)

Live Your Life Insurance (short primer on using Whole Life as your emergency/opportunity fund)

Busting the Life Insurance Lies (deeper dive into how Whole Life works, also has a story)

Busting the Retirement Lies (about 401k plans and options beyond retirement)

Busting the Interest Rate Lies (about mortgages and car loans, a young person's story)

Busting the Real Estate Investing Lies (about the importance of cash flow)

Perpetual Wealth (speaks about legacy beyond money and tells a story about three generations)

Busting the College Planning Lies (helpful for both parents and students)

Busting the Budgeting Lies (what to do for a spending plan that works)

Adventures at Prosperity Patch (children's book on prosperity thinking, featuring a dog and an alpaca)

For more info and to buy, visit ProsperityThinkers.com/shop.

BUSTING THE SCARCITY MINDSET

Your Guide to Becoming a Prosperity Thinker

Kim D. H. Butler
and
Kristen Hugins

PROSPERITY ECONOMICS MOVEMENT

Busting the Scarcity Mindset
Copyright © 2025 Kim D. H. Butler and Kristen Hugins

ISBN: 978-1-7375867-9-1

First Print Edition
May 2025

Produced in the United States of America

Prosperity Economics Movement
22790 Highway 259 South
Mount Enterprise, TX 75681
ProsperityThinkers.com

DISCLAIMER: Although the authors and publisher have made every effort to ensure that the information in this book was correct at press time, the authors and publisher do not assume and hereby disclaim any liability to any party for any loss, damage, or disruption caused by errors or omissions, whether such errors or omissions result from negligence, accident, or any other cause. This book is also not intended to provide specific financial or legal advice. The authors and publisher do not assume and hereby disclaim any liability to any party for any loss, damage, or disruption caused by the information in this book. For advice and guidance specific to your situation, please contact Prosperity Economics Movement or a qualified expert. If you do not agree to these terms, you may return this book to Prosperity Economics Movement for a full refund.

TRADEMARK NOTICE: Prosperity Economics, Prosperity Economic Advisor, and Prosperity Economic Advisors are trademarks of Prosperity Economics Movement.

This book was published with the guidance and services of Social Motion Publishing, which specializes in cause-related books. For more information, go to SocialMotionPublishing.com.

Dedication

This book is dedicated to Trey and Kaylea Berry, and Robby and Emma Butler, four people who live this effort daily in a way that I am so grateful for, and I can see the results in their lives. And to my Dad, Dan Hays, purchaser of the famed milk cow when I was in 4th grade, believer that all good things come to those who work on farms, and still serving student teachers in his mid 80s. Together, he and my Mom taught me and my sister how to Bust Scarcity Mindsets daily.

—Kim

For Kyler and Inara Hugins—you inspire me every day to live in a prosperous way. And for all future generations, may you Bust the Scarcity Mindset for good and live lives full of joy, peace, and purpose.

—Kristen

Contents

Foreword ix
A Note from Kim: The Power of 11 xi
Introduction xiii
Chapter 1—Proactive Gratitude 1
Chapter 2—Learn to Use and See Money as a Tool 11
Chapter 3—Create—In a Be, Then Do, Way 27
Chapter 4—Make It Personal: Match Money to Values 45
Chapter 5—Intentional Income Design 61
Chapter 6—Invest in Your Growth 85
Chapter 7—Collaborate for Exponential Increase 97
Bonus Chapter 8—Share the Love: Abundant Families and
    Relationships 111
Bonus Chapter 9—A Metaphysical Economy 127
Conclusion 133
Appendix 1—The Focus Wheel 141
Appendix 2—7 Principles of Prosperity 143
Appendix 3—Human Life Value Calculators and Explanation 145
Acknowledgments 155
About the Authors 159
Notes 161
Recommended Resources 167

Foreword

Busting the Scarcity Mindset: Your Guide to Becoming a Prosperity Thinker is one more book in the 100,000+ already written about money, so why take the time? What Kim knows and will teach you within these pages works and will benefit your life—I discovered this the day we met in 2005.

The financial and life principles Kim teaches and lives by will lead you to unwavering wealth and fulfillment. Your mission, if you choose to accept it, is to discover what she knows and then calibrate your life and finances accordingly. It all starts by turning that first page.

Patrick Donohoe, Author
*Heads I Win, Tails You Lose:
A Financial Strategy to Reignite the American Dream*
Founder and CEO of Paradigm Life and PL Wealth Advisors

A Note from Kim: The Power of 11

While we know that 1 + 1 = 2 in math, people often say 1 + 1 = 3 to indicate a multiplier effect of some sort taking place (two heads are better than one type of thinking). I've said for many years that 1+1 should equal 11, indicating an exponential multiplier effect that can happen when humans come together to do good work and include Father Mother God in the mix. This means they are listening, sharing, caring, removing their own ego, giving first, etc.

My husband Todd Langford, of Truth Concepts fame, and I are a good example of this. Every book I've written in the past (ten so far) is made better by Todd's calculators. He sees in numbers, I see in words. He learns by watching, I learn by reading. He is analytical, I am conceptual. When the two of us come together to teach a class, as we do for three days a few times a year called Truth Training, the attendees get the best of him, me and we. 1+1=11 because any concept I share is backed up by numbers he shares. So, because this is my 11th book, I ask you to consider as you read: How can you install 1 + 1 = 11 in your life?

Kim Butler, Author of 11 books
Founder of Prosperity Thinkers

Introduction

> "If we command our wealth, we shall be rich and free; if our wealth commands us, we are poor indeed."
>
> EDMUND BURKE

How to Become a Prosperity Thinker

Before we can change our actions to create prosperity, we must change our thoughts. In Wayne Dyer's renowned interpretation of The Tao Te Ching, *Change Your Thoughts, Change Your Life: Living the Wisdom of the Tao,* he wrote eighty-one essays on the eighty-one verses, sharing insights and actionable steps to bring them to life. He opens it with a quote from George Bernard Shaw: "Progress is impossible without change, and those who cannot change their minds cannot change anything."

It is only when we change our mindset, our way of thinking, that we can truly change our actions in a sustainable way. This is why I emphasize becoming a prosperity thinker above all. Once you are thinking from a prosperous mindset, you'll naturally act in ways that will bring about prosperity in your life.

Backed by Science

An article on cognitive science from *Psychology Today* titled "How Thinking Creates Your Reality" describes how our brains work and why our thoughts are the basis for our actions and our lives. Our thoughts create our beliefs, which then form the lens through which we filter everything in our environment. The author of this article states, "You are participating in creating your reality whether you know it or not. There is nothing magical or woo-woo about it. It is simply the way our brains operate. When you deny, reject, or are unaware of this, then you have very little power and will feel like the victim of your life. But with awareness comes choice. When you start to understand the process and make it work for you, now you are empowered to be in charge of the life you create."

There is scientific evidence in multiple fields such as psychology and quantum physics that validates this concept of our thoughts creating our reality. Therefore, it would reason that in order to create a more prosperous life, we must change our thinking first. But don't take my word for it. Experiment and try it out for yourself!

One tip for changing your thoughts consistently is to post affirmations in a highly visible spot that you would like to begin believing. For example, you might write on a post-it note: "Money flows easily and frequently to me," and post it on your bathroom mirror to read multiple times a day. Then start to notice how money is flowing easily and frequently in your life. Put the principles listed below into practice and watch how your life begins to transform.

The Role of Trust and Faith

When we are faced with a scarcity mindset—in ourselves or others—we may find it difficult to change our mindset to one of abundance, regardless of the scientific evidence or knowing intellectually that it will make a difference. This is where trust and faith come in. Whatever spiritual tradition you may follow, whoever you may view as your higher power, turn your faith over to them. Trust that your higher power will guide you, provide for you, show you ways to become more and more prosperous each day.

You are not alone. Great abundance takes great faith. Hebrews 11:1 of the NKJV of the *Bible* says, "Now faith is the substance of things hoped for, the evidence of things not seen." The beauty of faith is that when you lean on it, you manifest and demonstrate abundance in evidence of things *seen* as well. But it takes having faith in your higher power first. As a good friend shared recently, "expect pleasant surprises." Divine Love enjoys any chance to show off Her abundance.

Core Principles for Busting the Scarcity Mindset

In this book, we'll cover the seven core principles for busting the scarcity mindset. Below is a brief summary of each principle. Which one stands out most to you?

1. **Proactive Gratitude**: This principle is as simple as it sounds—yet can be hard to act on consistently until you've established a daily habit of gratitude. Being proactive about gratitude means creating an intentional practice of being thankful every time you give and receive anything. Make lists, speak it out loud, give freely. How could you uplevel your gratitude?
2. **Use and See Money As a Tool**: Understanding your relationship with money is the first step to seeing and using money as a tool. It is not a stagnant thing sitting in a bank account, but rather a tool capable of multiplying wealth

when mastered. Become a big picture thinker, cultivate contentment and then use money as a propeller to move you and your dreams forward. In what ways do you use money as a tool, and in what ways could you expand your view of it to use it more effectively?

3. **Create—In a Be, then Do Way**: When creating anything—a business, art, a family, wealth—it's important to focus on your being first, then your doing. Be present. Then examine your life using a tool like our Focus Wheel and determine areas of your life you want to focus on improving in order to make your vision a reality. Bring these to life by moving your money in ways that will support your being and doing efforts. Who would you like to be? And what do you need to do in order to become that person?

4. **Match Money to Values**: First, you'll want to identify your core values if you haven't already. Five is a great number you can easily remember. Then it's important to understand your Human Life Value (HLV), not just in terms of your life insurance amount, but in terms of how much value you will create while you're alive. Once you know your core values and Human Life Value, you can intentionally develop and share your talents and unique abilities in ways that increase flow. What are your top five values?

5. **Intentional Income Design**: Live by design rather than by default. Take charge of your income and learn how to generate new income streams and opportunities. This will provide stability and independence during unpredictable times. Explore our Maximum Potential Calculator to see how intentional income design plays out over your lifetime. How can you intentionally increase your income and

uncover opportunities you may not have seen before?
6. **Invest in Your Growth**: It is important to invest in yourself first before investing in anything else. Build your own skills and confidence, focus on the gains as you go, and pursue work you truly enjoy to constantly be growing. You are your most valuable asset, and expanding your abundance mindset through continual growth will pay dividends beyond your wildest dreams. What do you do to invest in yourself and your growth now?
7. **Collaborate for Exponential Increase**: We are better together, and the exponential results we can achieve are too! Opening your mind to new collaborations and partnerships is the first step. Being prepared to view each crisis as an opportunity for growth helps you thrive in the face of adversity. And lastly, asking for help in resolving issues gives others the chance to shine and connect with you. The impact you can make when you collaborate is up to 10x what you can do alone. How can you leverage your collective strengths by partnering with other people or organizations?

It is critical to remember that each of these principles require changing your thinking first, then acting in practical ways to usher in abundance. The last principle demonstrates how becoming a prosperity thinker can influence and benefit others around you in exponential ways. I believe we each have unique gifts to share in this life, and when we tap into our abundant, prosperous mindset in consistent ways, we naturally share our gifts more expansively, reaching and helping more people as we grow.

Creating Space for Abundance

When scarcity (of time, resources, health or wealth) is persistent, it's even more critical that we hold strong to an abundance mindset. Do not let fear, doubt or indecision cloud your judgment or thinking process as you move forward on a path of abundance. Stay clear and calm in your intentions for creating an abundant life for yourself and everyone around you.

There are dozens of small ways we can create space for abundance in our lives. Sometimes scarcity sneaks in when we least expect it simply because we didn't make clear space for abundance. Try clearing and cleaning a small physical space in your home where you want to bring in more abundance. It could be in your kitchen, your entryway, or even your bedroom. Where do you want to see growth and expansion?

When it comes to time, experiment with clearing off nonessential appointments or meetings on your calendar in order to make room for more abundant activities. If you aren't sure exactly what those are yet, just put a placeholder in that says, "Abundance!" Who knows what the universe will send your way in the form of a person, opportunity or idea at that time!

How to Use This Book

I want you to get the most out of this book that you possibly can. For each reader, that will look different. Are you looking for inspiration? Quick tips? Practical application of proven financial principles? True-life stories of people who have transformed their scarcity mindsets into abundance mindsets? This book has all of those elements. I encourage you to read (or listen) in the way that works best for you: from start to finish, jumping around to the chapters that most interest you, or a combination of both.

I've divided the book into seven chapters that break down the core lessons you need to learn and practice to become a prosperity thinker, plus two more bonus chapters. If you are brand new to the concept of transforming a mindset of scarcity to one of prosperity, I would recommend reading the book in the order it's written since it is designed to take you through the thought processes and practical steps in a logical way. If, however, you already understand and practice some of the concepts here, I invite you to skip around based on what you're most curious about.

In addition to books like this (both print and audible), it's always important to turn to a community for support and guidance when fostering and growing an abundance mindset. Surround yourself with people who nurture your abundance. I invite you to return often to our blogs, podcasts, videos and books to immerse yourself in prosperity and abundance thinking. Let's begin!

CHAPTER 1

Proactive Gratitude

"Are we really grateful for the good already received? Then we shall avail ourselves of the blessings we have, and thus be fitted to receive more."

MARY BAKER EDDY

Begin with Gratitude

Stephen Covey is famous for saying, "Begin with the end in mind." In order to bust a mindset of scarcity and become a prosperity thinker, we must begin our journey with gratitude. If we do not already feel grateful for what we have, we cannot make room for more. What we focus our attention on expands. If we want more wealth, time, freedom, etc., we must first express gratitude for the wealth, time and freedom we currently have.

There is a magical connection between gratitude and joy as well. When we feel grateful for what we have, a feeling of joy fills us up and helps us get through whatever we may be facing. Perhaps you are reading or listening to this book because you have very little and are at the beginning of a new growth journey. Or perhaps you have an abundance of wealth but find yourself dissatisfied or still wrestling with a scarcity mindset. Wherever you are on your journey, when you begin with gratitude, joy will meet you there.

In the article, "Holy Joy," in the C.S. Sentinel, Deb Hensley writes, "Joy and gratitude are best friends. I've seen them walking hand in hand down the street. Maybe you have, too. They walk in total safety together through dark places of fear. I've even heard them laughing at storms, confidently riding the fiercest winds with their other trusty companion—courage."

What are some practical ways we can proactively practice gratitude? Verbally saying thank you to others, listing five to ten things you are grateful for in a journal at the end of the day, and pausing to take a deep breath and mentally say, "thank you," in any given moment are all simple ways to consistently express gratitude. Your breath, your heartbeat, your ability to move, your income, your family, your home, your mindset – all of these are wonderful examples of things we can be grateful for.

One aspect of beginning with gratitude that is important to note is that it creates a foundation for future wealth. When we build a foundation using the solid rock of gratitude (much like the parable in the Bible), we have the support we need for increased financial abundance.

Evidence of how beginning with a grateful mindset forms this foundation showed up in a Wasabi Publicity email I received. They shared six of Ken Honda's money mindset New Year's Resolutions, including two that speak to the importance of gratitude as the foundation for wealth. Honda is Japan's #1 bestselling personal development guru and author of *Happy Money: The Japanese Art of Making Peace With Your Money*.

1. Say "Thank you" when spending and receiving money:

The positive energy of gratitude invites more Happy Money into our lives, so take every chance you get to show your gratitude! When money comes in, say "Thank you" (or, as we say in Japan, "Arigato"). And, when money leaves you, you can say "Thank you" again, expressing gratitude for how the money served you or what it is bringing to you now.

2. **Appreciate what you currently have:** Make a list of everything you currently have and love: It could be your partner, your house or your car, or smaller things, like the chair you're sitting on or a pen you enjoy writing with. Look at the list and feel appreciation anew for all you've attracted to your life. Doing this opens a door to the flow of Happy Money, because what you appreciate, *appreciates!*

I love the concept that what you appreciate, appreciates! We naturally attract more of what we focus on. There is a popular saying that goes, "Gratitude turns what we have into enough." The irony of this saying is that as soon as we feel it is enough, we are rewarded with more. As long as we are living with a mindset of lack, we will continue to receive and experience lack. The beautiful (and challenging) thing about this realization is that it is all up to you—only *you* can change your mind.

Notice Abundance

In his list of money mindset resolutions, Honda continues with a third:

3. **Adopt an abundance mindset:** You can choose any mindset you wish, so why not choose one that maximizes your life's potential? We've been taught that money is scarce, that we have to get it before someone else does. If you adopt an

abundant mindset — believing there is more than enough for everyone — you see new possibilities, become more creative, and free yourself to create your own destiny.

But how do we adopt an abundance mindset? We've established that we must begin with gratitude. Secondly, we must notice the abundance in our lives. This involves expanding our awareness and vision to see abundance in all its many forms and manifestations. These may show up as opportunities, introductions, a check in the mail, wisdom you read, food on the table, and kindness from a stranger. The ways abundance reveals itself to us are infinite. Not merely limited to the material, it can be observed and experienced physically, intellectually, emotionally, and spiritually.

One obvious form of abundance is gifts. It is important to always be grateful and gracious when receiving gifts. This fuels a sense of abundance. However, some gifts may be perceived at first as challenges. Sometimes we learn best when we see the opposite side of the lesson or point that needs learning. That too, can be a gift.

Right around the time I read Matt Ridley's book, *The Rational Optimist*, my husband, Todd Langford of TruthConcepts, and I attended an Alpaca show. We didn't own any Alpacas yet, and we would attend shows where owners displayed their animals and the amazing sweaters, scarves etc. that people had made with the Alpaca fiber. This was a small show, on a cold day. Not a lot of people were in attendance at the time, and over in one corner were a variety of very colorful sweaters hanging up in a booth with a man standing nearby.

We walked over, and he immediately began expressing concern that people were "taking his wife's ideas" (since she had designed the sweaters). His conversation was exactly the opposite of what noticing abundance is and does for you. We literally wanted to run from his booth. I have never forgotten how sad that situation was, how I felt in the presence of serious scarcity being voiced, and how I wanted to share with him that he was hurting sales with his mindset.

Using that example, how can we learn to reframe a scarcity mindset into an abundance mindset? That man could have instead been delighted to see that people loved his wife's ideas so much that they were copying them. There is room enough in this world for infinite creative expression, and just as money must flow freely to grow, so must creativity. In this case, adopting an abundance mindset instead of a scarcity one would have increased this man's wealth directly (and increased the happiness of everyone who visited his booth).

In her book, *The Jewel of Abundance: Finding Prosperity through the Ancient Wisdom of Yoga*, Ellen Grace O'Brian writes, "When we're down and depressed and can't see much good anywhere—that experience will tend to compound itself." (p. 240) This seemed to be exactly what that man was going through. What is the way out of this spiral then when we find ourselves in it? Gratitude. When we acknowledge what we can be grateful for in any situation, we adopt an abundance mindset. This shifts our thinking from scarcity to plentiful good, and we naturally begin to see and experience more prosperity.

Give Freely (or Give First)

There is significant value – both to others and to yourself – in giving freely and first. Giving is gratitude in action. It is saying, "I have more than enough. I'd like to share with you." This is true for money, time, physical gifts, mental focus, labor, and more.

Why is it important to give freely? When we give freely, we don't expect anything in return. Our motives are generous and open, with no attachment to outcome. This, in turn, frees us from any expectations we may have about what is done with the gift or whether it is appreciated. It also frees the receiver from any strings attached, which is a great kindness. That free-flowing energy can be felt and creates a stronger connection between the giver and receiver.

Giving first means we prioritize giving. However, in order to give first, we must have an abundance mindset. Otherwise it may be done begrudgingly. When we truly value giving over holding on tight to our money, we create a win-win situation. Money is a tool, and if it is not given freely and first, it is difficult for it to flow and be used in the most effective ways.

Can you think of a time when you prioritized giving a gift over spending on yourself, worrying about money or saving it? How did it feel? What happened after you gave the gift?

The act of giving transforms consciousness by affirming we are all connected and here to help and support each other. O'Brian writes about how giving freely and joyfully yields abundance:

"In our less-inspired moments, we may operate under the notion that as we grow in faith, we will develop a more giving consciousness. Or that we will give when we have more material resources at our disposal. That's a classic mistake. Through giving we affirm our abundance. When we refuse to give, we refuse our own prosperity. What's the formula? Give what you can. It's as simple as that." (p. 250)

I recall a time when cash flow was tight. (Remember cash flow issues don't go away, they just get bigger zeros on them!) It was tight enough that I was not buying anything extra, and I felt really restricted. I am fine not buying personal things, like clothes and fun food, yet I get quite frustrated when I can't spend money on my business. I knew that I needed to get money moving again.

Money doesn't serve us when it is stuck. This is true whether it is locked up in a retirement plan or sitting behind some mental wall. I knew this intellectually, yet I was having trouble putting it into practice. Then I saw an ad for Heifer International. My family had a long relationship with donating to them. It started when an elderly friend gave my children $3 chicks as Christmas gifts every year. Yes, three dollars, and yes, a chicken! The actual chick was given to a family to grow, lay eggs, and get them out of poverty. I had always loved Heifer's method of "Teach them to fish." So I jumped on their website and donated $25. It was money I thought I didn't have at the time, yet I recall that being a turning point in that particular "cash flow crunch."

Since then, I've adopted the mantra, "give first." This kind of thinking causes breaks in log jams of apparent discord. It opens up your mindset to new possibilities and helps you think more creatively and expansively.

There is significant scientific evidence that shows that giving activates our brain in positive ways. In a University of Arizona article titled, "Understanding the Brain Science Behind Giving and Receiving Gifts," Associate Professor of Psychology, Jessica Andrews-Hanna, says:

"There is a decent amount of research showing that the act of giving actually makes us feel better. Evidence from brain imaging also suggests that both giving gifts and receiving gifts activate core areas of our brain associated with reward and pleasure. These brain regions also stimulate the neurotransmitter dopamine. All in all, psychology and neuroscience suggest that giving gifts to other people can be a very rewarding phenomenon that can bring happiness to ourselves and others."

She goes on to discuss how giving can motivate the receiver to want to pay it forward and give themselves. Looking at the big picture, it's clear that giving freely and first as a habit can do wonders not only for our own wealth and well-being, but for the wealth and well-being of society as a whole. Giving connects people, affirms abundance and inspires even more giving.

It's important to note that giving does not have to involve material wealth or gifts. While material gifts can be fun to give and receive, giving your time, energy, or even a compliment are all wonderful gifts as well. Giving any amount of anything you can give freely will yield positive results and increase abundance.

Uplevel Your Gratitude

How can you uplevel your gratitude? Here is an example: I love Emma Dawg, our Great Dane. She is physically beautiful, well disciplined and well behaved, soft to pet and fun to be around. These are all physical or material qualities. I like to uplevel them by taking each one and upping it a notch to a spiritual, or metaphysical, quality.

Physical beauty is also expressed in Love and Emma is a Dog who loves first (as most dogs do!). Her self discipline or ability to do what I ask of her is an act of obedience, demonstrating self control and a desire to please, both inspirational qualities. Her softness (to me) and enjoyment of petting (to her) can appear to be very physical, yet what do they represent spiritually? They are the essence of relationship and caring, fostering a win-win-win environment, a give-first attitude, and an inner feeling of joy and happiness. That is how you uplevel your gratitude.

Questions for Reflection
- What are you grateful for today?
- Do you have a daily gratitude practice?
- Where do you see abundance in your life?
- What could you give today?
- What person or organization would you like to give to?
- How could you make giving a regular habit?
- How have you seen giving improve your wealth and well-being?
- How might you uplevel your gratitude?

Quick Tips for Proactive Gratitude
- **Just start!** Find one thing or person to say thank you to or about. Say thank you to God for the sunrise this morning. Or say thank you to your dog, child, or spouse for sharing their life with you.
- **Be proactive by thanking someone *before* you receive something.** We are not giving thanks expecting anything to come back to us. We also don't express our gratitude to get recognition or kudos. We give thanks to show our appreciation for someone and their generosity, regardless of the end result.
- **Write a handwritten thank you note** and put it in snail mail. Everyone loves to get a handwritten thank you note—it's so rare! I guarantee it will be cherished.
- **Write thank you notes with your children** to show them how to do it and teach them the skill. The younger the better! Even if all they can do is scribble, that's a great start!

CHAPTER 2

Learn to Use and See Money as a Tool

"Money is only a tool. It will take you wherever you wish, but it will not replace you as the driver. It will give you the means for the satisfaction of your desires, but it will not provide you with desires."

AYN RAND

Each one of us holds a different view of money in our mind's eye. This is often based on how our parents perceived and used money, or how we felt money may have influenced us and our families. In order to see money objectively so that we can effectively use it as a tool, we must examine—and in some cases unlearn—our old beliefs about money.

In my own experience, a couple years ago we had some green years in business. We were sitting on some extra cash, and I was getting excited about our next investment. It became very clear we needed to rebuild the dam on our property that makes our lake. We had to use all of those extra resources to literally put dirt in the ground. It was very tempting to be frustrated about this. We could've gone on a trip, made an investment, done a hundred other things than put dirt in the ground.

The bulldozer came, and shoved dirt in the holes of the dam. With weather and time, it became a pretty big project. It came to me at some point that we were shoring up the dam for the next generation. My kids' kids were going to benefit from this work. It was such a powerful adjustment in my thinking. It took something that was day-to-day thinking and literally stretched it out a hundred or more years. And it took negative thinking and transformed it into gratitude that we got to do it, had the lake, and found the right person to do the work (which took almost a year).

Once I was clear that positive things were occurring, it was clear that money was a tool here to have a massive impact on our whole family and extended generations instead of just a selfish use. Therefore, the money expanded the opportunities for our family and loved ones for generations.

It's still very appealing to many people to store money. But this was going directly against that. Instead of making a financial investment, we got to fix the dam which was a different kind of investment. It helped me stand up for one of the principles I preach: flow, as in cash flow (dollars coming and going) versus storing money for someday.

To Love or Not to Love Money: Understanding Our Emotions & Triggers Around Money

"For the love of money is the root of all evil: which while some coveted after, they have erred from the faith, and pierced themselves through with many sorrows." —1 Timothy 6:10, *King James Version of the Bible*

When we see money as a tool, it creates space between us and the money itself. For example, a hammer is a tool, and as such, we do not love it, not in the deepest meaning of love that we may feel for another person. We may like the hammer and what it does for us, but that is different than loving it.

As a result of this perspective, we are less attached to money, and we do not "pierce [ourselves] with many sorrows," as the Bible quote above says. Being unattached to money itself or the outcome of its use prevents us from experiencing an emotional rollercoaster. We are free then mentally to adapt and use money *in the way that provides the most value*. Perhaps one of the greatest benefits of seeing money as a tool and not loving it as such, is our ability to pivot when needed and change the way we use it.

However, while this may sound good in theory, it can be difficult to put into practice. Mindsets rarely change overnight! The transformation of a scarcity mindset into a prosperity one often begins when a person realizes *why* they believe what they believe and makes a conscious choice to either accept that belief or change it.

I highly recommend taking the Wealth Dynamics Quiz at wealthdynamics.geniusu.com in order to better understand your mindset around and current relationship with money. This quiz helps you learn more about how you see and use money, and how to work with your strengths through eight profiles. Knowing your strengths when it comes to money can be especially helpful when working with others. The quiz also recommends the wealth profiles that are most beneficial for you to seek out and work with in order to amplify your results—in business and in life.

Through collaboration, we can multiply our money much faster and maximize our impact (see Chapter 7 for more on this concept). Understanding ourselves and our current relationship with money is essential to overcoming any negative biases, unfounded beliefs, or even misplaced love of money. Then we can focus on the mindset we want to have about money going forward.

All actions regarding money—earning, buying, investing and donating, to name a few —begin with emotion. This is yet another vital reason to understand your emotions around money and what triggers you may have when it is time to take action. It is important to ask yourself:

- Why do I want to take this action?
- What is the best outcome? What is the worst? Am I okay with either?
- Is a love of money getting in the way of making a sound decision?
- What emotions do I want to feel about this situation?

Knowing you possess the power to change your mindset around money is the first step. It brings awareness to your emotions. Instead of judging yourself, just try observing what you feel when you receive a bill, pay for a service or look at a financial statement. Noticing the feelings you have can help you understand that you are not your feelings (or your thoughts), and you have the power to change them.

Using money as a tool is most effective when we are operating from a place of awareness. Our motives must be pure and clear. When we are unaware of our emotions surrounding money, we may use the tool incorrectly or for ulterior motives. In order to act from a place of integrity with our money, we need to know why we are employing it and, ideally, have transparent intentions.

When we say one thing and do another with our money, we are letting an underlying scarcity mindset rule us. And money, as the tool, will simply do whatever we direct it to do. It does not have an opinion—or an emotion, for that matter—about what we do with it or what outcome it creates.

As a practical way to begin breaking down your own emotional barriers around money, take five minutes to journal about your personal and professional history with money. Try a creative approach and write from the perspective of money, the tool. For example, your journal entry may begin with something like, "When you were five years old, you put me in a piggy bank where it was dark and I felt stifled and useless." Taking this alternative perspective will help you see how you have used money as a tool in the past and identify ways you'd like to change your use of money in the future. Ready, set, go!

Now that you've seen what your past use of money was like from the tool's perspective, how do you want to change your use of it as a tool? What might you do differently with money in the next year? How will that impact your emotions about money?

It is inTeresting to note that data collected from law firms show that 20-40% of all divorces are due to financial problems. Our closest relationships are deeply affected by our emotions around money and how we use it as a tool. If we could see it more objectively and clearly as a tool that is here for us to wield, would we take the time and devote energy to learning how to use this tool more effectively?

The first two Principles of Prosperity we teach at Prosperity Thinkers are: **Think and See**. They both align perfectly with this concept of understanding our emotional triggers around money. They state:

- **Think**: Owning a prosperity mindset eliminates poverty; scarcity thinking keeps you stuck.
- **See**: Increase your prosperity by adopting a "big picture" perspective in which you can see how each one of your

economic decisions affects all the others. Avoid financial "tunnel vision."

When we think with a prosperity mindset and see money with a big picture perspective as a tool that helps us achieve our goals, we are free to grow in all ways. Our perceptions of money are powerful. When we know how to change them to benefit ourselves and others, we can change our lives, and ultimately, the world we live in.

Cultivate Contentment

In addition to adjusting our perception of money as a tool, it is vital to how we use it that we *first* cultivate contentment. That's right; contentment is not the *result* of using money as a tool, but a *prerequisite* for using the tool of money correctly. Why?

If we do not first feel content (a synonym for "content" may be "grateful"), we are at risk for misusing the tool of money and compromising our integrity in the process. Beginning with the false premise that money will bring us contentment is a trap many fall into time and again. However, true contentment comes *before* the growth of money, not after. It is a constant, unchangeable state of mind we can access at any time.

Contentment is simply defined in the Merriam Webster dictionary as "satisfied." When we are satisfied with what we have, we are prepared to receive more. Some may view contentment as complacency. However, I believe that true contentment is a natural driver of growth. It does not leave us sitting on our laurels, stagnating or waiting. It is a peaceful state of mind that is akin to happiness, but more steady and consistent.

When we are satisfied, our shoulders relax, we exhale, and we see the people and world around us with grateful eyes. It is this perspective that allows room for growth. Contrary to a dissatisfied state of mind in which one is always hustling, grabbing, desperate and uneasy, contentment provides peace and attracts similar energy.

A friend of mine once shared with me how unhappy she was in her search for love and a fulfilling relationship. She was simultaneously dissatisfied with her work and income. In an effort to satisfy both of those desires, she fell hard and fast for a man who portrayed himself as a wealthy provider who would take care of her and her children. Unfortunately, only one year into their marriage, it was clear that his words and actions did not line up.

Upon reflection, she realized she had attempted to circumvent her own values by putting money first. Not only that, but she had handed over her own power tool of money to her partner, and his lack of integrity had left them in a lurch. In this case, she thought marrying this man and giving him control over her and her family's financial abundance would bring her contentment. Instead, it brought the opposite—much dissatisfaction and disappointment.

If she had cultivated contentment first, then it would have been easier for her to see through the false image he was portraying. She would not have mistaken his promises for truth. Already feeling content, she wouldn't be nearly as smitten with his money and the life she thought it would afford her. It is a common story for many, simply told with different characters. We may easily get duped into thinking money can buy us love, security, or contentment. However, when we prioritize being content first, when we use money as a tool, it will only expand our contentment in the right direction.

How can we feel content though when we do not have what we need? I want to be clear that contentment does not equal poverty. In fact, it is the opposite. When we cultivate contentment as a mindset, we are living in our *full abundance*. The material picture surrounding us may look and feel like it is lacking, but as soon as we cultivate contentment, we find we are provided for in extraordinary ways.

As Paulo Coehlo wrote in *The Alchemist*, "And when you want something, all the universe conspires to help you achieve it." (p. 22) Feeling content and wanting something are not mutually exclusive. We can hold them both in equal weight, and when we understand how to use the tool of money, we will witness our desire transform into growth.

So how exactly do we cultivate contentment? Here are three tips for starters:

1. **Beginner's Mind**: Close your eyes and take 3 conscious breaths, inhaling and exhaling deeply. Then open your eyes slowly and see your surroundings as though you are seeing them for the very first time. What do you see? How does it make you feel?
2. **Origin Story**: Choose one thing in your daily life and trace it back to its origin. For example, if you love your cherry wood bed frame, contemplate how many people and resources it went through to get into your bedroom. This creates a deeper appreciation for the things in your life and connects you energetically to all those who created them.
3. **Practicing Presence**: Take off your shoes and walk barefoot on the earth. Feel the soil or grass underfoot, the breeze on your skin, the sun on your face. Notice how the earth supports you. Listen to the birds singing. Inhale the fresh air. Become so grounded that the present moment is all there is. Let everything else —worries, plans, thoughts—fall away.

When cultivating contentment in these ways, we find peace in the ordinary, the everyday moments that string together to make a life. From this basis, we can use money as a tool to create whatever we desire that aligns with our purpose.

In addition to cultivating contentment for ourselves, it is doubly meaningful to cultivate it for others. Money is an ideal tool for doing so. Perhaps you own a business and are creating jobs, or you multiply wealth through investments and give to charities, or you work at a job you love and provide for your family.

There are infinite possibilities for how we can use money as a tool to cultivate contentment for others. The key is in *how* we use it. As mentioned in Chapter 1, giving freely is the only way to truly give. When we model cultivating contentment for ourselves *and* use money as a tool to share what we have learned with others, we exponentially increase the contentment in our communities and the world at large.

Conscious capitalism is a philosophy and movement that can create contentment on a communal scale. Investopedia.com defines conscious capitalism as "a socially responsible economic and political philosophy." The concept was created by Whole Foods co-founder, John Mackey, and author and marketing professor, Raj Sisodia. The whole premise is that businesses should operate ethically while pursuing products and taking into account all parties involved, including employees, humanity and the environment.

When we run and support businesses that practice conscious capitalism, we cultivate contentment on a larger scale than just ourselves. We have a choice every day of where and how we will put our money. Making it a tool for good ensures growth on more than just the financial level.

The third and fourth Principles of Prosperity we teach are: **Measure and Flow**. These are critical to cultivating contentment because they emphasize awareness of opportunities, opportunity costs and prioritizing cash flow. We can only be aware of these when we are already content and allowing growth of money to flow.

- **Measure**: Always measure your opportunity costs—what your dollars could earn if you did not spend or commit them elsewhere. Awareness of opportunity costs enables you to recover them. Ignore this at your peril.
- **Flow**: The true measure of prosperity is cash flow. Don't focus on net worth alone.

When we are content, it is easier to measure opportunity costs objectively and not get caught up in emotional attachment to purchases or investments. It also feels more natural to witness the flow of money when you're already content. Envision yourself sitting on the solid bank of a river, watching the water flow by. Instead of damning the river with beliefs of lack or hoarding, you can observe the flow and let it happen.

Use Money as a Propeller to Move You Forward

When it comes to cash flow, imagining money as a steadily flowing river is helpful. However, when you want to imagine your money moving *you* forward and experience the *velocity*, or speed, of money as I've coached clients on for years, you can think of it as a propeller. When you see money as a propeller, the sky is the limit. Your options are truly boundless.

But how exactly does a propeller work? And how is money similar? An article on propellers from the National Air and Space Museum says, "Think of a propeller as a spinning wing. Like a wing, it produces lift, but in a forward direction—a force we refer to as **thrust**." When used with the last three prosperity principles—Control, Move and Multiply—money can work for you just like a propeller does. It can be your spinning wing that produces lift, or increase, in a forward direction. The key is in knowing *how* to control, move, and multiply your money.

First, it's important to know which direction you're headed. Otherwise money can propel you towards things you don't actually want. Where do you want your money to take you? What is your dream life? Who are you becoming?

I learned this lesson of using money as a propeller early in life. My sister had gotten a cow, and we had gotten a milking machine. Together, we started selling the extra milk. For $1 a gallon (3 cups of which was cream), people could get fresh milk out of the extra refrigerator in our garage or the cooler we drug to church every Sunday and Wednesday. I've estimated we each made around $25,000 during Middle and High School.

We were definitely using money as a propeller. Making all that money taught us so many valuable skills that would propel us both forward in life. I had to keep good records for 4-H, so I learned bookkeeping. I had to buy my own cows, grain, hay, choose the bull, feed the calf milk from a bottle, continue to prepare for the county and state fairs, all the while playing sports and keeping up good grades. (Poor grades simply are not an option when you have a teacher and a principal for parents.) I think this is how I learned to read quickly.

My environment supported me using money as a propeller too. Our family only watched Disney on Sunday night. The TV was never on any other time. We were either outside working or inside reading, studying, or sleeping. I won some major events at the fairs so I learned to win graciously, just like I'd had to learn to lose graciously. All the while, I learned to dig positive lessons out of both positive and negative events. There is no point being mad or frustrated while trying to get a 1500 pound cow to do what you want instead of what it wants. I kept my focus on the work at hand and the money I was making to keep hitting my goals as I grew.

The propeller of money will thrust you forward whichever direction your controls are telling it to go. This is why your mindset is so important. If you are thinking with a scarcity mindset, you will likely not think far enough ahead or will underestimate what you and your money are capable of. However, with an abundance mindset, you can soar above the clouds easily towards a destination you are worthy of.

Through your money flight, it's important to keep checking and tracking your course, just as you would in a plane. Kristen had the opportunity to co-pilot a plane recently with a friend, and she was astonished at how the smallest turn of the wheel or adjustment of the controls would quickly change their trajectory. This is a perfect metaphor for the powerful difference small adjustments in your mindset can make. You'll also want to add practical tools (just like tools you'd have to use to assist with flying an airplane) that can help you check and track your course along the way. Some examples of helpful money tools may be: software, regularly scheduled meetings with key people, automated savings or investments, ongoing education about finances, etc. As you learn more, you can adjust your course to align with what you've learned.

Much like money, a propeller moves the plane (your life) where you direct it. It doesn't have a mind of its own. It is simply a tool, a part of the plane, to get you from point A to point B. You can land and take off again and again. You can change course at a moment's notice.

Kristen shared that one of the most fascinating things about a propeller when she witnessed it up close, in action in the co-pilot's seat, is that *you can't see it when it's in motion.* It moves so fast it becomes invisible to the naked eye. What would happen if you could direct your money to work for you and thrust you forward at a speed like that?

"If everyone is moving forward together, then success takes care of itself."
—Henry Ford

Like a propeller, money is meant to move people and ideas forward. It only stagnates if no one is flying the plane. Own the fact that you are the pilot of your own life. And money is a critical tool you can use to propel yourself and others forward.

Taking the metaphor one step further, imagine if you were in charge of a fleet of planes. With dozens of propellers in the sky (your money multiplied many times over), think of how much more you could accomplish, how many more people you could take with you where you're headed. Through multiple investments, compound interest, and using money as a tool time and again, the velocity of money will work for you so one dollar thrusts you ahead dozens of times instead of just once. Eventually the speed will become so high that you won't even see it working. You'll just know that your money is always working for you, taking you where you want to go.

As mentioned earlier, the fifth, sixth and seventh Principles of Prosperity are: Control, Move and Multiply. When you control your finances, move them in the direction you want to go, and multiply your money rapidly, you will find yourself on the fast-track to wealth.

- **Control**: Those with the gold make the rules. Stay in control of your money rather than relinquishing control to others.
- **Move**: The velocity of money is the movement of dollars through assets. Movement accelerates prosperity; accumulation slows it down. Avoid stagnation in assets where dollars accumulate but are not put to use.

- **Multiply**: Prosperity comes readily when your money "multiplies"—meaning that one dollar does many jobs. Your money is disabled when one dollar performs only one or two jobs.

With a scarcity mindset, your control of money will be limited, it will feel difficult for you to move it, and multiplying it will be near impossible. That's why it's vital that you shift your mindset to one of abundance by seeing and using money as a tool, and propel yourself into a financially abundant future.

Questions for Reflection
- What triggers do you have around earning, spending, investing or saving money?
- In what ways do you use money as a tool, and in what ways could you expand your view of it to use it more effectively?
- Is your money in your control? If not, what small step could you take to regain control of it?
- Where do you notice your dollars accumulating (slowing down) in your life? Where could you move your dollars so they will speed up growth?
- What are a few of the jobs one dollar does for you today? What ideas do you have for multiplying each dollar's jobs?

Quick Tips to Use and See Money as a Tool
- **Brainstorm five creative ways** you see money as an idea first.
- **Laugh about money!** When we can have a sense of humor about money, we engage with it more freely. For example, my nephew, Cole, helps us with social media, and in one of his searches he found an old DuckTales video of Uncle Scrooge teaching his nephews—Huey, Dewey, and Louie—

about money, and it is Prosperity Economics to a tee. The transcript is brilliant! It's from the 1980s and we laughed out loud!

- **Visualize money in your hand, your wallet, and your bank account.** You can think about anything you want. Even though you may not know how to utilize money as a tool yet, you can visualize money and what it can do for you. You may not be able to utilize it until you can see it. *"Our eyes only see and our ears only hear what our brain is looking for."* —Dan Sullivan
- **Invest in yourself in a small way.** Go slow, start small. Buy a $20 book (like this one that you bought - way to go!). Then notice how in doing so, money served as a tool for your growth. (Learn more about investing in yourself in Chapter 6.)

CHAPTER 3

Create—In a Be, Then Do, Way

> "The secret of living fearlessly is stillness. The process of transformation requires inner discipline to focus the mind on whatever we're doing, and perseverance until we begin to change from the inside. We might call this process 'The Art of Becoming.' In the heart of stillness lies the key to lasting meaning and joy."
>
> DEVI, "THE ART OF BECOMING"

The Importance of Presence

The title of Ram Dass's classic book from 1971 states the first principle of creation: *Be Here Now*. Being present is essential to creating anything because it ensures that we are starting with a *present moment mindset*. If we begin with a past mindset, we will recreate the past. If we begin with a future mindset, we may overlook important information in the present that could hold keys to our success in the future.

Being present, often referred to as mindfulness, requires staying fully engaged with the current moment. This practice can have profound benefits that will directly impact your ability to create.

Here are five reasons why being present is essential to creating:

1. **Improved Mental Health**: Being present helps reduce stress, anxiety, and depressive symptoms. By focusing on the here and now, we are less likely to dwell on past regrets or worry about the future, leading to a calmer and more peaceful state of mind. When we are at peace, we create from a clean slate.
2. **Better Relationships**: Presence allows for deeper and more meaningful interactions with others. This is key to finding quality people who can help you make your creations a reality. When you are fully attentive in conversations and interactions, you foster stronger connections, better communication, and a greater sense of empathy and understanding.
3. **Increased Productivity and Focus**: Mindfulness enhances concentration and focus, allowing for better performance in work and creating wealth overall. Being present helps minimize distractions and enables us to fully engage with the task at hand. This leads to higher quality outcomes and efficiency.
4. **Greater Enjoyment and Satisfaction**: Engaging fully in the present moment enriches experiences, whether it's enjoying a meal, spending time in nature, creating something purposeful, or participating in hobbies. This heightened awareness can elevate our enjoyment and lead to greater overall satisfaction.
5. **Intentional Decision Making**: Being present helps us make more thoughtful, informed decisions. By focusing on the current situation and tuning into your emotions and thoughts without the clutter of past experiences or future anxieties,

you can evaluate options more clearly and make choices that are aligned with your vision for what you are creating.

Cultivating a habit of being present can enhance your overall well-being, transform your interactions with others, and exponentially improve your ability to create wealth.

Be, Do, Have is a concept that my friend, George Huang, taught me long ago. This is our goal in terms of the order we live in. But people often want the sequence to be: Have, Do, Be. They want to have things before doing what's necessary, or being who they need to be in order to do and have those things. However, because "being" starts with our mindset, it is relatively easier to take action there than in the doing part. We can't "do the doing" until we "be the being."

George Huang first connected with me when he learned about my work in one of Robert Kiyosaki's recordings back in 1998. A fellow entrepreneur and coach, George is the author of the book *Financial Statements Made Practical: A Step-by-Step Visual Guide*. A former plastic surgeon, he now coaches entrepreneurs on how to become more profitable.

I asked him to share his perspective on the Be, Do, Have concept because he was the first person to introduce me to it in a clear way. He said, "In our Western culture, there's a lot of emphasis placed on what we do, what action to take. And you do have to take action. We can *observe* someone taking the action, however, and there's a different energy behind it in different people. That difference is in your inner guidance system. That's the human *being* part of things. When we take action that's aligned with who we are, we're more likely to get results that are constructive. We are also more able to be resilient and flexible in dealing with the challenges we inevitably face along the journey."

George also shared that we tend to trust people with whom we resonate. Sometimes we can be fooled, but for the most part who we resonate with stems from who we are being at our core. Who we surround ourselves with makes a big difference in how present we are in any given situation. When we trust the people we are with and feel trusted by them, we feel free to be ourselves. We feel like we belong.

When it comes to a goal or vision we have, what's big to one person may be small to another. Everybody has their own dreams. Wherever each person is on their path to their dreams, there's a presence. It can be a shrinking presence, a powerful presence, or even a magnetic presence. What presence are you bringing to your work, your family, your friends, your dreams?

In addition to who we surround ourselves with, the world at large—and how we translate it—can make a big difference in our being. George pointed out as we were talking about this chapter that two people may interpret the same event very differently. It's important to question how we're translating what we're picking up in the world through our thoughts and actions. That can greatly influence our sense of being.

When busting the scarcity mindset, where are you coming from? What are your thoughts and feelings? What's their decision-making matrix?

Because freedom is one of George's values, he said, "If something gives me freedom, sign me up. If there's no freedom, I'm not interested." Everybody has a different set of decision-making patterns and preferences largely based on their values. They all contribute to who we're being.

The challenge is knowing yourself well enough and trusting your inner guidance system enough that you can live authentically, being who you are. A lot of us compensate and try to be someone we're not because we think that's what we need to do to survive and advance. In survival situations this may be necessary, but most of us do not live lives of mere survival.

It can be easy to get caught up in the busyness of doing a million things. As George reminded me, "We are human beings first, not human doings." Because we do have things to do in this life, the doing is important. Yet based on George's experience, he's found, "The things you *do* have more power when they come from who you're *being*."

George's story elucidates this concept beautifully:

"When I was seventeen, I visited my brother, who was training in Neurology at the Mayo Clinic in Rochester, Minnesota. I was a high school senior waiting for him in the library, and a giant oversized book found me from across the table. I was fascinated because I had never seen an oversized book before. It turns out it was a book on plastic surgery—before and after.

It wasn't the cosmetic side that appealed to me; it was the reconstructive plastic surgery side. I saw some really gory pictures, and I instantly knew that's what I wanted to do when I grew up. I didn't know it would take fifteen years of schooling until I could make that dream come true. At age thirty-two, after many twists and turns, I was practicing as a newly minted plastic surgeon. Very quickly, I realized I was a business owner and didn't like it. There were a lot of regulations and ongoing battles with insurance carriers. Eventually, I was doing a lot more cosmetic surgery than reconstructive surgery. That's not who I was at the core. I didn't go through all that schooling to become the world's best cosmetic surgeon. I genuinely longed to do the reconstructive side.

At my core, I wanted to help people restore function, and recover from illness, injury, or disease. There was a soul dissonance for me the longer I performed cosmetic surgery. I got paid more than I would have for reconstructive surgery, but it felt like it was eroding my soul and sucking the energy and life out of me to do something I didn't want to do.

My wife said to me, 'If you keep going like this, you're going to die an early death (that was in 2001)." So when our second child was born, I told her, "I don't know what I'm going to do next, but I'm out of here." A lot of people said ending my cosmetic surgery career took a lot of courage, but I felt like it would've been harder to keep doing something that didn't resonate with my soul. I also figured I could find other ways to be useful.

Being true to your "being" is an ongoing process of self-reflection, self-discovery, and reinvention. I do think that at the core, there are immutable values that stay constant. I'm a big believer in listening to one's inner guidance system and trusting the process.

Sometimes you may find yourself wondering, what have I gotten into? Why did I make these decisions? No matter what path we take, those doubts are going to come up. I'm a big believer through experience and observation that we have the greatest chance of making it through life's challenges, and leading a fulfilling life, when we can be authentic and honest about who we are. I equate the word, "being" with values, our inner guidance system, and being authentic. Much like the Inuits have twenty ways of describing rain, there are over a dozen ways we can describe "being."

I think challenging one's beliefs and challenging one's scarcity results, if you will, are important. You can have a mindset mixture: a prosperous and growth mindset in one area of your life and a fixed and closed mindset in another area. I think the challenge in life is seeking to identify those blind spots where we harbor scarcity thinking and action-taking. Is it easy to identify those blind spots and do something about them? No, but I do think that's the goal. Otherwise, you're going to just keep getting what you've always gotten.

After I ended my plastic surgery career, I thought I was going to set up a seminar business with workshops to support parents and teachers to raise children who are financially aware. It went nowhere really fast. Most parents had to figure it out for themselves first; they weren't ready to raise financially aware kids because they weren't being financially aware themselves.

Two years into it I wasn't making any more money, just spending money. I lost my confidence, but I knew I didn't want to go back to plastic surgery. Just because I'm trained to do it doesn't mean that it is the thing to do. Then, I discovered that working with entrepreneurs was fun. I help them start or grow their businesses to be more profitable and boost cash flow. That means addressing their marketing, sales, financial picture, etc., but it's more holistic in nature. Along the way I developed software that helps the business owner or advisor bring together sales and marketing data with financial data to see how that matches up with their goals so they can make appropriate data-informed decisions. As a plastic surgeon, I was trained to operate head to toe and learned to see in four dimensions, so that's how I naturally look at business now."

The following are two practical steps and mindset shifts George recommends to cultivate this mindset of being, then doing:

1. **Start by being naturally curious**—about how things work, including yourself. What makes you tick? Perform thought experiments, different ways of looking at life and appreciating what you have.

2. **Challenge your beliefs**—ask, "does that really make sense now?" This way of being, this approach to life and problem-solving, does this work now? If so, keep it. But if not, try something new. It can be uncomfortable to try something new even when intellectually we know it might be better for us. We have to be able to work through that discomfort to get through to a more expanded version of who we are. A lot of people get scared when they feel uncomfortable.

Being, Then Doing

In our modern culture, we often do the reverse of what George shared above and prioritize doing over being. It takes a level of intention and discipline to focus on "being" first. This is much more effective than focusing on "doing" first because it centers us on what matters most. When we are grounded in our "being," any action we take from that mindful place will be aligned with our own motives, goals and values.

One of the ways many people focus on being is through meditation. Eileen Luders, a researcher at the Department of Neurology at UCLA's School of Medicine has discovered evidence that meditation changes the physical structure of the brain. As the article, "Your Brain on Meditation," in *Mindful* magazine states, "Like anything else that requires practice, meditation is a training program for the brain. 'Regular use may strengthen the connections between neurons and can also make new connections,' Luders explains. 'These tiny changes, in thousands of connections, can lead to visible changes in the structure of the brain.' Those structural changes, in turn, create a brain that is better at doing whatever you've asked it to do. Musicians' brains could get better at analyzing and creating music. Mathematicians' brains may get better at solving problems."

In short, we can train our brains to get better at anything with focused attention. For example, if we want to be more resilient in the face of adversity, we can meditate on acceptance. If we want to improve our concentration, we can focus on the breath or a candle flame. If we want to experience more abundance, we can focus on gratitude. Being present and focusing on the here and now helps us improve our overall awareness and bring what we want to create into existence.

Pastor Chuck Swindoll shared a beautiful insight on the difference between being and doing in one of his daily devotionals, "Doing vs. Being," on his website, Insight.org:

"Doing is usually connected with a vocation or career, *how we make a living*. Being is much deeper. It relates to character, who we are, and *how we make a life*."

When we prioritize who we are over what we do, we can make a life we are proud to live. As a creator—of a business, a work of art, a family, a home, a life—we each have a responsibility to create our own being first. Only then can we create from an authentic place of integrity and produce meaningful results.

If the first step to creating wealth is being present, where are you now?

I've provided a couple tools in the following pages to help you get present to your current reality. Prosperity is about measuring progress. In order to create the life we desire, we need to have an accurate picture of where we are now—and a greater vision of where we are headed. Using the Focus Wheel, measure your level of satisfaction in each area to assess your current situation in these core areas:

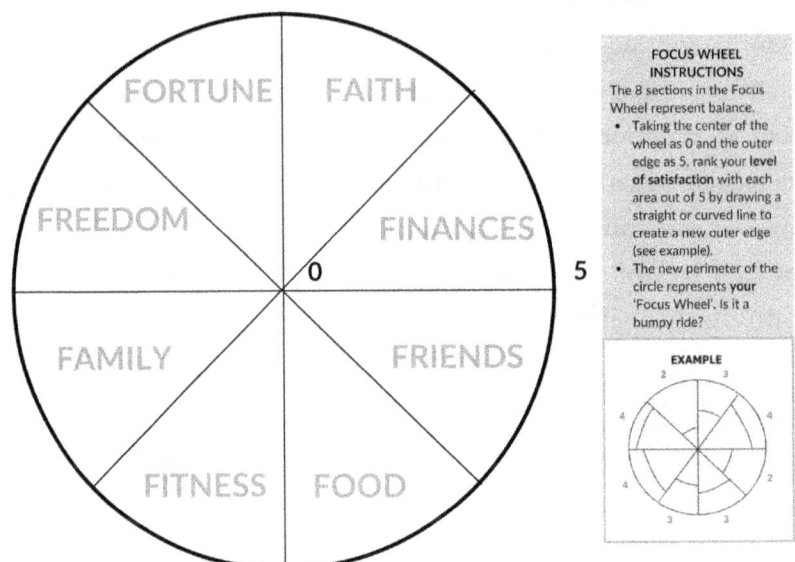

(See Appendix 1 for a larger version of the Focus Wheel.)

Next, write out your ultimate vision for each focus area using the table on the opposite page. Think big! Imagine your perfect day and what each of these areas would look like. For example, you may see yourself: reading a spiritual book, receiving large payments for your work, seeing friends for a delicious, nourishing lunch, taking a yoga class with your significant other, feeling free to do what you want all evening and noticing the fortune of new opportunities and connections throughout your day. Make it personal to you. There is no judgment here; remember, the sky's the limit!

Lastly, on the following page, list out a habit in each area below that you want to add or strengthen in order to get you to your ultimate vision.

Once you've established your baseline, your vision for where you are headed, and the new habits you need to get there, you can visioneer your future.

FOCUS AREA	ULTIMATE VISION
Faith	
Finances	
Friends	
Food	
Fitness	
Family	
Freedom	
Fortune	

FOCUS AREA	HABIT TO ADD OR STRENGTHEN
Faith	
Finances	
Friends	
Food	
Fitness	
Family	
Freedom	
Fortune	

The baseline you've detailed in your Focus Wheel is your current state of being. As my friend, George, brought to light, once you establish a solid foundation of *being*, your *doing* becomes more focused and impactful. What future will you create for yourself and the people around you?

Keep Your Money Moving to Serve Your Being and Doing
One question I have always been passionate about pursuing is: how can the velocity and flow of money serve your being *and* doing? First, it's important to note that we must make room for money to flow. This could mean clearing physical space, opening up our minds to new ideas, or removing obstacles to financial growth. While some people are prone to accumulating and saving money, keeping it moving will actually better serve your sense of purpose. Stagnant things don't grow; dynamic things do.

To effectively keep your money moving and serving both your being and doing aspects, it's important to consider how your financial activities align with your broader life goals and values. Here are a few ideas of how you can keep money moving to support both your present awareness (being) and your future aspirations (doing):

1. **Strategically Allocate Your Resources**
    Budget for both mindfulness and growth: Allocate funds for activities that enhance your present awareness and personal growth, such as meditation courses, yoga classes, or spiritual retreats. These investments help nurture your "being" by fostering a deeper sense of inner peace and mindfulness.
    Invest in your goals: Channel a portion of your finances into investments or savings that fund your future goals. Whether it's saving for a home, investing in education, or

starting a business, these actions support your "doing" by building a foundation for future achievements.

Maintain flexibility: Keep some of your resources fluid to allow for spontaneous decisions that can lead to personal enrichment and joy, embodying the balance of being present while also planning for the future.

2. **Use Financial Tools to Enhance "Being" and "Doing"**

   Automate savings and investments: Use financial tools that automatically route a predefined portion of your income to savings and investment accounts. This not only simplifies the process of securing your future but also helps you maintain peace of mind in the present.

   Engage with a trusted financial strategist: Regular consultations with your financial strategist can help you stay aligned with your financial objectives without getting overly consumed by the mechanics of financial planning, thus supporting your "being" mode by reducing stress.

   Embrace technology: Utilize apps and online platforms for managing your finances (such as Currence, which I highly recommend!) which can provide insights and track your progress towards both immediate and long-term financial goals, supporting your active "doing" efforts.

3. **Periodically Review and Adjust Your Financial Strategy**

   Reflect on personal values and goals: Regularly assess the areas of the Focus Wheel to determine whether your spending, saving, and investment choices align with your evolving personal values and life goals. This ensures that your finances are not just a means to an end, but a living, moving part of a fulfilling life journey.

   Adapt to life changes: Be prepared to modify your financial plans as your life circumstances and goals change. This may involve shifting funds between different accounts, changing investment strategies, or reallocating budgets to better serve your current needs and future ambitions.

Balance risk and reward: Consider different financial strategies that balance risk and reward according to your age, responsibilities, and life aspirations. This helps nurture your "being" by minimizing anxiety over finances, while energizing your "doing" mode by actively engaging in growth-oriented financial practices.

It's important that your financial decisions and actions enhance your ability to be fully present in the moment while also efficiently working towards future aspirations. This dual focus on "being" first, and "doing" second, can significantly boost your overall life satisfaction and well-being.

Some more practical steps you can take to cultivate a mindset of "being," then "doing" include: annual strategic planning, quarterly goal or objective setting, and regular visualization exercises to envision the life you are creating. Taking a few deep breaths or doing a short meditation before any of these activities can help you drop into your authentic self and act from a clear mindset of possibility.

Just like returning to the breath in meditation when you catch yourself caught up in your thoughts, returning to "being" before "doing" will be a constant, repetitive process. Challenges and setbacks may derail you temporarily, but you can always start again. Our "being" never goes away. It's just our awareness of it that shifts.

When you prioritize presence, be, *then* do, and keep your money moving, you create from a place of purposeful power. When you center yourself in your authentic being, what you create will make a bigger impact than you could any other way.

Questions for Reflection
- Who would you like to be?
- What do you need to do in order to become that person?
- Are you focused on being, doing, or having right now? Which one appeals most to you?
- When is a time in your life you have been centered in your authentic being? What actions did you take immediately following?
- What things/experiences/relationships are you focused on having at this time in your life? (There is no judgment here, just self-observation.)
- How could your "being" support you in doing the things you need to do?
- How could your "doing" get the things you want to have?

Quick Tips for Creating—In a "Be," Then "Do" Way
- **Start a spiritual practice.** If the word "spiritual" doesn't work for you, use the word "inspirational." Feed your mind every morning with something spiritual/inspirational—a book, song, guided meditation, prayer, or podcast. Make sure your spiritual practice is helping you become your future self.
- **Write down three things you are feeding your brain**, and pay attention to what those are creating in your life. Seek brain food that creates the type of person you are aiming to become, the future self you want to be. Pay attention to the source of information and what it's doing to how you are being.*
- **Figure out how you learn best.** Do you like to read, watch, listen, or get your hands on things? I asked a 45-year-old

man the other day how he learned best, and he didn't know. The term creating indicates newness. As human beings, we are either growing or dying. If you want to be working on your future self, making your life better, improving how you are being, you always want to be creating. Your body is always creating. Our cells regenerate every seven years, and our thoughts should be equally creative. We should be creating with our thoughts to pull us forward into our future self space where we can grow, improve and be better. We need to create in our minds before we can do it in any other form. Everybody is creative. It's *how* we create that is unique to each of us.

Pro tip: Stay off the mainstream news. I get my news from only two positive sources: *The Christian Science Monitor* and *The Good News Network*. I trust that any bigger, immediate news will be communicated to me by friends or family when I need to know. This helps me focus on what I can control and not get caught up in a scarcity mindset.

CHAPTER 4

Make It Personal: Match Money to Values

> "You can only become truly accomplished at something you love. Don't make money your goal. Instead, pursue the things you love doing, and then do them so well that people can't take their eyes off you."
>
> MAYA ANGELOU

As you create wealth for yourself and your family, it's essential to match your money to your values. Knowing your values and aligning with them is important at all stages of money growth and management: your earning, investing and spending. By making your wealth creation personal, you make it purposeful.

Identify Your Values

The first step to matching your money to your values is taking the time to identify your values. As we covered in Chapter 2, money is a tool. Therefore, your values are the motivating force behind that tool, putting it into motion.

You may already have a clear idea of your core values. However, if you don't, below are several examples of core values to get you started. I recommend narrowing down your list to your top three to five core values in order to simplify and focus your money management around those. Which ones resonate most with you? (This list is just a starting point; there are many more!)

1. **Integrity:** Adhering to moral and ethical principles, being honest and fair.
2. **Respect:** Valuing others, treating everyone with dignity and consideration.
3. **Responsibility:** Being accountable for your actions and duties.
4. **Compassion:** Showing kindness, empathy, and a willingness to help others.
5. **Courage:** Facing challenges and taking risks despite fear.
6. **Commitment:** Dedication to a cause, goal, or relationship.
7. **Innovation:** Valuing creativity and the pursuit of new ideas and solutions.
8. **Excellence:** Striving for the highest quality and continuous improvement.
9. **Sustainability:** Focusing on long-term environmental, social, and economic health.
10. **Community:** Prioritizing social connections, collaboration, and contributing to the well-being of others.

Identifying your values is essential for aligning your financial decisions—earning, investing, and spending—with what truly matters to you. When you reflect on your financial experiences and consider what brought you the most satisfaction or discomfort, what do you notice? Which values come to the forefront?

For instance, think about a job that made you feel fulfilled or a purchase that brought long-term happiness. What value comes up strongest?

Then recall times of financial stress or regret in order to reveal values that were compromised. Which values did you compromise? Journal about these experiences to help you pinpoint the values underlying your feelings. This process can guide you toward more value-aligned financial choices in the future.

Examining the financial habits of your role models can also provide valuable insights into your own values. Consider why you admire certain people's financial decisions and what qualities they exhibit, such as generosity, careful discernment, or ambition. These admired traits can shed light on your own financial values.

You may also find clarity in discussing your values as they relate to your financial decisions with trusted friends, family, or mentors. These discussions can offer new perspectives and help you clarify your values. People close to you might notice patterns in your spending, saving, and investing behaviors that align with specific values you hold dear. It is always easier for others to see our patterns than it is for us to see them.

Lastly, prioritizing and testing your financial values in real-life situations can further refine your understanding. Take your list of values related to financial decisions and rank them by importance. Post them where you can see them on a daily basis, ideally in a location where you make financial decisions. Then, make conscious efforts to align your earning, investing, and spending habits with these values.

For example, if you value security, focus on building a robust emergency fund and making conservative investments. If generosity is important to you, allocate a portion of your budget to charitable giving and set up automatic monthly donations. By observing how you feel when your financial actions align with your values, you can make more informed and fulfilling decisions.

Still unsure what your top values are? Tammi Brannan, my sister, runs a business in which she helps people identify their values on a daily basis. She recommends jotting down answers to the following questions to further narrow in on your top values:

- Tell me the roles you play in your life and the things that make up your day. What do you have to have to feel successful and effective in that role and activity?
- What can you *not* get enough of? (passions)
- What things would you sacrifice or risk for?
- What things would you dedicate all your resources to, whether you were paid for it or not?
- What could you do for a very long time without losing energy?
- What do you find yourself constantly wanting to teach or share with others?

Ultimately, your habits, behaviors and actions determine how your values play out in the world. In James Clear's book, *Atomic Habits*, he discusses "the habit loop" of cue, craving, response, reward. The first phase, "cue" (a.k.a. trigger), is the most important for starting a new habit. When it comes to creating new habits to align your financial decisions with your values, you want to make it as easy on yourself as possible to make a change. Enter the "cue," your secret weapon to getting a new financial habit to stick.

According to Clear, cues include: time, location, preceding event, emotional state and other people. For example, if you want to begin a habit aligned with your value of innovation, you might tap into cues that could help you build a new business or invest in a startup. Say you wanted to dedicate two hours a week to this new venture. You could use a time cue, such as the same day and time each week, to do research, make calls or attend a networking event. Or you could find an accountability partner (other people cue) to meet with you for those two hours each week and brainstorm together. When we intentionally build a new habit by using a cue that works for us, we set ourselves up for success.

One way we might identify our values is through examining habits we have and paying attention to how we feel after we do those habits. I've had many experiences in my life where I realized my habits were out of alignment with my values and made minor changes that produced big results.

For example, I spent my early adult life in Scottsdale, AZ getting my hair, nails, and more done for my own self care. But then a friend added up how much I had spent on my nails in a year, and it totaled almost $3,000. I realized spending that amount on nails was not aligned with my values. I decided right then and there that that was not a good use of $3,000 for me. I have no judgment of others who want to do that, but for me, it was not in alignment with my values.

I wanted to use my money as efficiently as possible. I had goals, objectives, and desires that were way more important than having my nails done. So I quit having them done immediately, and I've never gone back. It's not that I would never get them done again (especially for a wedding or special event). It's just that I had gotten clarity on my values and how I wanted to direct my money in better alignment with them. Afterall, not only was I spending money on my nails, I was also spending time getting them done—over an hour every other week. What else could I do with that time?

On the flipside, I discovered a value of mine that resulted in me spending more money. Eating healthy is very important to me. I'm careful not to go overboard, but I will spend money without regard to the cost for food and snacks that are healthy for me. This can include extra fruits and vegetables as well as higher quality red meat. I will spend money on those items because they are important to me.

The value here for me is physical health, which translates into mental health and energy as well. I try not to overthink it. I don't want to be so overtly focused on what I'm eating that I'm obsessed about it, while at the same time I know that there is nothing as valuable as feeling lean and being mentally sharp. Feeling lean requires certain eating habits. Does that mean I never eat ice cream? Heck no! I absolutely eat ice cream. But the value of feeling lean and being mentally sharp is so important to me that I will think about what I put in my mouth *before* I put it in there. Because of that value, I choose to automate what I eat as much as possible beforehand. The things that are important to us we need to automate. If we want to have healthy snacks, we need to automate ordering them. If we want to save money, we need to automate that. If we want to feel healthy, we need to automate healthy habits.

Another one of my values is reading. I'm happy to spend as much money as needed to read books. My Kindle bill is pretty high. Before Kindle existed, I was happy to buy books at the store. I've given a lot of books away, but I still have a lot. I feel like reading is super important. Even if it's your third learning modality (behind watching and listening), it's so important to learn how to do it.

I had a stepson who flat-out refused to read. I kept persisting with him. We had a nightly reading routine for a while. At some point he pulled out the *Lord of the Rings* game manual, and that's what he wanted to read. I said, "Awesome, let's do it!" Mind you, I do not like games or *Lord of the Rings*, but I read *The Lord of the Rings Manual* with him so he could see I was in this space with him, supporting him. That went on for a couple months. Then he got over his hangup and was willing to read other things. It truly didn't matter to me what he read, I just wanted him reading. It was a joyful experience because I met him in the middle.

If you want to gamify identifying your values and your family members' values, I highly recommend a couple card games that help create values orientation:
- *The Values Cards* by Marie McNamara and John Veeken
- *Family Legacy* by Kim Butler; great for ages 6+, simple family game
- *The Quiet Year* by Avery Alder

If you're having a hard time matching your values to your money, do the following:
- **Get clear on your own values.** Play one of the values games above. Keep in mind that values change; today I spend less money on my material items than I have previously in my life because I live on a farm. Thirty years ago, I lived in Scottsdale, AZ, and I spent more on certain things that mattered more to me then.
- **Be purposeful with your spending.** Make decisions with your brain on. We get into serious default mode. When you realize something you're spending is out of alignment with your values (which I will admit is hard to know when you're younger), make a change in your spending. Self-knowledge is something that takes time on this earth to occur.
- **When you become aware something is out of alignment, ask yourself: why?** Are you trying to keep up with the Joneses? Your parents? Your spouse? Then try to just stop the spending cold-turkey. With my nails, I just canceled the appointment and never went back. Sometimes it's easy; sometimes it's not. I spoke with one client who spent so much on clothes she couldn't save any money. I told her not to buy anything. She called back three months later and said

she hated me for that recommendation, but she is so glad I made her do it because it worked!
- **If cutting spending is not feasible, try to add a positive habit.** Let's say that you are really stuck with that classic $7 latte every afternoon. It's become a habit. Don't try to take it away first. Just add another positive habit. What I mean by that is buy cut vegetables at the store with a little bit of a treat (like cheese or ranch dressing or something to make the veggies more exciting), and add the habit of eating the vegetables before the latte. So when the latte desire kicks in, you already have veggies in your stomach and aren't as hungry for the latte. Add the habit so you're focused first on what you're adding, not on what you're taking away. Refer to James Clear's habit stacking in *Atomic Habits* and BJ Fogg's *Tiny Habits*.
- **Celebrate!** That doesn't mean go get a latte! What it means is something else positive: add fruit to the vegetables. Notice I picked vegetables first. Or think of some other healthy thing you can add. Maybe instead of a quick 10-minute walk (which is a great celebration), it's a 15-minute walk (to somewhere other than Starbucks). It doesn't have to be a material thing you add, but it can be. When you do a whole month of a new habit, then add something to celebrate—even a one-time thing is great. I celebrate with ice cream all the time. Scott Donnell, creator of *Value Creation Kid*, says, "Until further notice, celebrate all progress."

Your Human Life Value: Big Picture

When we think of values on a macro level in the financial world, we cannot help but think about your Human Live Value (HLV). This is a helpful method for determining the maximum amount of life insurance you can have, taking into account factors like: income, retirement age, taxes, expenses and inflation rate. It asks the question, "If you were to die, how much money would it take to replace the economic value you bring to your family?"

Human Life Value uses your current income to predict your future earning potential, and therefore, can fluctuate year to year. While you can calculate it yourself to determine your maximum insurance amount available, I recommend working with a professional to fully understand your Human Life Value. For a quick snapshot of your Human Life Value, you can use an online calculator like the one at the website of the nonprofit organization, Life Happens: LifeHappens.org/human-life-value-calculator.

However, I like to think of your Human Life Value as more than a number you calculate to determine maximum insurance amounts available for when you die. Your Human Life Value is equal to your life's work. In other words, the value you possess and create in your lifetime is the most meaningful work you do. Value can be defined in a variety of ways, not just financial, though that is an obvious way to measure it. It may also be defined by the number of lives you touch, the impact you make, the creativity you express, and the love you give and receive.

That said, numbers are a logical way to measure value because it is easy for the human mind to understand. Quantifying value makes it tangible. As an exercise in visioning your future and focusing more on the living aspect of your Human Life Value, I encourage you to write out your goal for your Human Life Value in terms of dollars as an experiment. I recommend breaking it down into three to five major goals that will all add up to your total Human Life Value dollar amount at the end of your life.

Dream big! What is each goal worth once completed? If you want to write out another value metric (i.e. # of people impacted, # art pieces created, etc.) next to the dollar value, go for it! The more specific you can be, the better. You can always change these goals and values over time.

Feel free to fill in the chart below or copy it into your own notebook. This can also be easily done on a spreadsheet if you prefer. Then you can update it year to year as your goals evolve.

Life Goals	$ Value	Other Value
1.		
2.		
3.		
4.		
5.		
TOTAL Human Life Value		

If you find you are resistant to placing a dollar value on your life goals, and your Human Life Value as a whole, I encourage you to face that resistance. Explore it. Perhaps reread Chapter 2 on seeing money as a tool to reconsider your perspective and learn new ways of looking at money. In the end, placing a dollar value on your big life goals, and ultimately your Human Life Value, will help you hone in on the value you are going to create for others. It is a service to all the people who will benefit from your value to do this exercise, you included.

This more expansive, futuristic way of thinking about Human Life Value is intended to help you narrow in on what you truly value in life and how to better align your money with your values *while you're alive.*

Life Insurance and Your Human Life Value

When it comes to life insurance, Human Life Value is the maximum amount of Life Insurance that you can have on your life, all totaled up: group Insurance, whole life, term life, and different companies. It is very important to know this maximum number, even if you choose not to insure it.

The rules of thumb are usually ten to thirty times income, depending on age OR 1 x gross worth, especially if you are older and wealthier. If you are a stay-at-home parent, typically your Human Life Value is one half of your spouse's. And children are typically one quarter of the higher earning parent's Human Life Value.

It is very important that life insurance agents offer Human Life Value, (the maximum Death Benefit) even if their client doesn't take it, otherwise the agent is contributing to them being under-insured. While talking about cash value is much more fun, the fact is, death is a guaranteed event and should be insured.

Remember, insurance is designed to replace something, in this case, an income stream, or the services a non-working parent provides. Most often, Human Life Value is a mix of group insurance, term insurance and whole life insurance.

So if the insurance company thinks you're worth that much, then you're worth that much. While that is your economic human life value, it's difficult for somebody who makes $150,000 to see a need for $3 million in death benefit at twenty times earnings, right? They say, "I don't want to leave him or her rich when I'm gone."

What I will tell you is you cannot leave anybody rich with life insurance. The best you can hope to do is replace a person's economic Human Life Value, and only if they don't expect any substantial raises along the way. All you can get is still going to be less than what it's going to take to replace their income.

To see more of what that looks like and put it into perspective, check out the Human Life Value calculations in the Appendix.

The key thing to remember is we're replacing human economic value. It's not a license to spend. It's important that the family understands how this works, so that they don't go on a spending spree when a Death Benefit is paid to them in a lump sum.

Sharing Your Values Through Your Talents

Now you've identified your core values, created new habits to align your financial decision-making with your values, and expanded your thinking with a broader understanding of your Human Life Value. This is the part where you get to live your values.

On a daily basis, the path to a life of purpose is one on which you continually share your values through your talents. What talents and skills do you possess that are natural avenues for your values to shine?

Tammi Brannan, my younger sister by three years, paid for school by milking cows like I did. We both learned early on the important lessons hard work can teach us. If anyone understands how to share your values through your talents, it's Tammi.

In 2007, she created a business custom-designed around her philosophies and talents called Blueprint Process, where she listens to clients go through the process of discovering their God-given talents. Primarily using her own intuitive process and philosophy, she helps people do work they believe in. If her clients have already taken other assessments when they get to Blueprint, such as Kolbe, CliftonStrengths, and Dan Sullivan's Unique Ability, she'll incorporate those results as well. "When we do work we believe in, we are using our talents," Tammi says. "If we believe in our values and convictions, heart and soul, our talents will naturally be employed."

If you're working for an organization you actually believe in, you believe in the work they're doing and your values are involved. But if you're not actually jazzed by the actual activity, that might be a poor fit, and you might want to go to the higher ups to seek a better role. When you use your God-given talents, energy infuses your system. It's important that your work brings you energy instead of waiting for the weekend, or vacation, or retirement. Tammi says, "Love your work so much that you're not looking forward to anything; you're fully present in that moment."

Tammi's Blueprint Process is predicated on the belief that each one of us is equally valuable, and we come ready-made to identify our purpose. What did you come ready-made with? Her process, as well as most assessments, goes so far beyond work. If you were made with these qualities and passions to do certain things, wouldn't you want to use them and do those things all the time?

According to Tammi and her research, your purpose is timeless and not role-specific. She's always translating what she learns about people into their various roles as parents, employees, entrepreneurs, or spouses to help them live by utilizing their gifts in a well-rounded way. She felt led to her work while on a cruise at the interior passage of Alaska, in a wild and raw environment. It was the first vacation she'd been on that she didn't want to end. It was a defining moment for her, and she began a journey of self-study. At the time, she was a mom, wife and worker bee, and she felt she had very little control over her own choices.

Prior to the trip, I had spoken with Tammi about her helping me and my clients with the question of purpose. That started the entrepreneurial wheels turning and planted a seed of purpose for Tammi as well. She helped me and my clients for a while, then she started her own business. She now has thirteen practitioners working under her helping clients.

A lot of the assessments out there are based on other people's opinions of you, your role, etc. Tammi primarily studies what is eternal, constant, and unchanging in a person. She helps people study their values, passions, skills, and purpose. Those four categories make up the toolbox of one hundred items she studies with her clients. The first half of her process is research, while the second half is application. Without awareness of how to align our values with our talents, we can't use them.

No person's blueprint is the same as another. Going through the Blueprint Process is a validating experience—unearthing the bedrock of who you are and learning how to be that unapologetically. When someone is standing more strongly on their blueprint, their alignment of values and talents, they own it. Old patterns, people and things that no longer work for your life fall away and new ones are built.

Tammi warns that when you operate outside of your blueprint, you work much harder and way more inefficiently than you should. When you stand strongly on your blueprint, that becomes more obvious. You start drawing support for the projects that don't fit you. It all happens very naturally. The overall consequence is that people are working more efficiently and effectively with more peace and greater joy.

It's bizarre, because for example, you'd think to gain more success as a business owner, often the paradigm is that in order to grow the business, you're going to have to work harder, longer hours, and spend more money. With your blueprint, you will often let that fear go. When you share your values through your talents, it feels easy and effortless. You have more confidence, courage, and you take risks with more boldness.

As Tammi says and models through her own work, "Moving

from scarcity to abundance is recognizing your God-given talents and then using them."

What do you notice about the velocity of money when you are aligned with your values? When we are in a flow state, using our talents for good in a way that feels personally fulfilling, there is usually a sense of ease financially. Scarcity naturally becomes a thing of the past, and we find ourselves standing strong in the middle of a rushing river of abundance, wealth flowing to, through and from us. People line the riverbanks of our life, to support us, magnify our impact and receive all the good we have to give.

Questions for Reflection

- What are your top five values?
- What can you share with a family member about Human Life Value?
- Which assessments are you interested in taking to learn more about your values, passions, and talents?
- If you had to rate yourself 1-5 (5 being the highest) on how you're doing with aligning your values to your talents, what score would you give yourself?

Quick Tips for Matching Money to Values

- **Narrow down your values**. Go find a list of values on the web (or use our list here), then narrow it down to twenty, then ten, then ideally five. Write the five values that speak to you on a post-it note. Put them somewhere you will see them every day: your wallet, your bathroom mirror, your fridge. Start making money decisions based on these values.
- **Make a mindmap on a piece of paper or using Miro.** Draw a circle. Put your values on the outside and elements of your

life on the inside and draw lines where those connect. Use color. Write ideas for elements you'd like to add to your life in a different color and connect those to your values. Creating a visual map helps you start to think differently about how to apply your values in your life.

- **Start living your values.** Start small. Choose one of the values on your post-it or mindmap and live it a little bit more thoroughly this week. Notice when you have a choice to make and you can honor that value.
- **Get specific in applying a value.** The more specific you are, the better. You can apply math to money, so you can be very specific when it comes to money. Let's also get specific around what you value. That's why we narrow them down to a small number—ideally five. Take each value and try to apply it. The more specific you get, the better results you will get. The more you narrow in, the easier it is to say no to all the things that don't fit that value. For example, if you value community and you have a choice to either go to a movie or volunteer at your local soup kitchen, choose the soup kitchen because it aligns with your value.
- **Make a list of three ways you can demonstrate a particular value.** Try not to limit yourself to material demonstrations of the value. Your list can include ways that are thought-based or expression-based. What can you do in your mental space that will align you better with your values without spending money? This is a great opportunity for creativity.

CHAPTER 5

Intentional Income Design

> "Many people take no care of their money till they come nearly to the end of it, and others do just the same with their time."
>
> JOHANN WOLFGANG VON GOETHE

In today's changing economy, the concept of intentional income design is essential to finding your independence from fluctuating trends and circumstances. By actively shaping how you earn and manage your income, you can bust the scarcity mindset and create a life that aligns with your values and goals. In this chapter, we will explore three aspects of intentional income design: increasing your income, seeking opportunities, and setting your own rules of engagement.

However, the first step mentally is to let go of a scarcity mindset when it comes to income, and commit to taking charge of your income creation—today. Afterall, if we do not build intentional income by design, we will take what we get by default. Default mode operates at the lowest common denominator of our current awareness of money and what's possible. Whereas, design mode says we are creators who can design exactly what we want our income to be. Rather than living by default, we choose to live by design.

How to Increase Your Income

The first step towards intentional income design is to identify ways you can increase your income. Each way below, as well as any you may brainstorm on your own, comes with its own set of challenges and rewards. It's important to choose an income increasing strategy that feels true to you and your values.

One simple strategy to increase your income before implementing one of the strategies below is to start with putting all your income into a separate account, then only putting into your checking account what you want to live on that month. This way, you consciously and intentionally separate income from expenses by design.

Below are a few strategies for increasing your income you may consider:

1. **Investing in Education and Skills Development:** Investing in yourself is one of the most reliable ways to increase your earning potential. This can mean pursuing higher education, obtaining certifications, or developing new skills relevant to your industry. For instance, if you're in the tech industry, learning a new programming language or mastering data analysis can open doors to higher-paying positions. Online platforms like Coursera, Udemy, and LinkedIn Learning offer affordable courses that can enhance your resume and increase your marketability. Ultimately, YOU are your greatest asset. No one can take your education away from you, and the skills you develop expand your ability to earn as well as your confidence and perception of your own capabilities.

2. **Exploring Side Hustles:** Side hustles have become a popular way to supplement primary income. From freelance writing and graphic design to ride-sharing and selling handmade goods online, side hustles provide additional revenue streams. Websites like Upwork, Fiverr, and Etsy can help you get started. Side hustles not only boost your income but also allow you to explore your passions and hobbies in a financially rewarding way. Whether you're looking for a side hustle or a new main hustle, an article we found titled "16 Remote Jobs That Pay at Least $40 Per Hour" from Yahoo Finance is worth checking out (see Notes for details).
3. **Negotiating Salary and Benefits or Increasing Your Rates:** Many people undervalue the power of negotiation. Whether you're starting a new job, seeking a raise in your current position, or looking to raise your rates in your own business, negotiating can significantly impact your financial situation. Research industry standards, prepare a compelling case for your worth, and practice negotiation techniques. Putting the time in upfront will yield great results in the long run. Employers and clients often expect negotiations, and advocating for yourself can result in better compensation. You can easily earn 10% more (or a bonus of 10%) if you do something that goes the extra mile such as: bring new ideas to your boss or client, offer to do some extra work above and beyond, or bring in new business even if that isn't your main role.
4. **Passive Income Streams:** Creating passive income streams is a key component of intentional income design. It's not truly passive as the phrase implies, however it can produce

results that make income-earning much easier in the long run. Passive income requires upfront investment of time, money, or both, but it continues to generate revenue with minimal ongoing effort. Examples include investing in dividend paying stocks or cash flowing real estate, creating and selling an online course, or earning royalties from creative works like books or music. The goal is to build assets that work for you, freeing up your time and energy for other pursuits.

Seek Opportunities

"The secret of change is to focus all of your energy, not on fighting the old, but on building the new." -Socrates

To design your income intentionally, it is important to actively seek out and capitalize on new opportunities. This involves staying informed, networking, and being open to new possibilities. It can be tempting to fall into old patterns or beliefs of scarcity, but I encourage you to embrace your new mindset of abundance and use it as your mental foundation to build upon. So many of us get caught in old income models and may even waste energy fighting those old models. Instead, as Socrates advises, put your efforts on building the new. And when it comes to opportunities, that requires having the vision and openness to see new possibilities where others may not.

Here are four ideas for seeking opportunities to get you started:

1. **Networking:** Building and maintaining a robust professional network is crucial. Attend industry conferences, join professional associations, and engage on social media platforms like LinkedIn. Networking not only exposes you to new opportunities but also allows you to learn from others'

experiences and gain valuable insights into your field. Strong professional connections can lead to job offers, collaborations, and mentorships that propel your career and business forward. When networking, place a special focus on listening for opportunities and asking questions of others that will open doors for both you and the other person. This is a skill that takes practice and discernment, but it is well worth the investment once you master it.

2. **Staying Informed:** The world is constantly evolving, and staying informed about trends in your industry and the economy at large can help you identify opportunities. It can also make you much more interesting to talk with at networking functions! Subscribe to industry publications, follow thought leaders on social media, and participate in webinars and workshops. Being knowledgeable about the latest developments enables you to anticipate changes and adapt your income strategies accordingly.

3. **Being Open to Change:** Flexibility is key when seeking opportunities. Sometimes, opportunities come in unexpected forms. Being open to change and willing to take calculated risks can lead to significant rewards. This might mean switching careers, relocating for a job, starting your own business, or exploring a new avenue for investing. Embrace change as a chance to grow and be open to the possibilities you encounter on a daily basis.

4. **Leveraging Technology:** Technology has democratized access to opportunities. Platforms like LinkedIn, Glassdoor, and Indeed make it easier than ever to find job openings and connect with employers. Additionally, online marketplaces like Amazon and Shopify allow individuals to start

their own businesses with relatively low overhead. Utilize technology as a tool to discover and pursue opportunities that align with your income goals. If learning and using technology tools feels difficult for you, consider hiring an assistant or asking for help from a co-worker who can leverage technology and get the results you are looking for more quickly.

What other ways can you open yourself up to new income generating opportunities?

Set Your Own Rules of Engagement

Designing your income intentionally also means setting your own rules of engagement. This is your life and your income creation, not anyone else's. Setting your own rules involves defining how you want to work, what you value, and what boundaries you need to establish to maintain a healthy work-life alignment.

The tips below will help you set your own rules of engagement. These are especially important to write out and post where you will see them daily. That way, you will follow your own rules and ask others to do the same. Think about your rules of engagement as the banks of a river. It is important to have sturdy banks so the river doesn't flood or get off track. Eventually it will become second nature for you to operate within those rules, and your increased income will flow freely within the firm boundaries you've set for your rules of engagement.

1. **Define Your Values:** As covered in the previous chapter, understanding what you value most will guide your decisions and actions—both in your personal and your professional life. Do you prioritize flexibility, creativity, financial security, or work that makes a positive impact? Knowing

your values helps you make intentional choices about the types of work you pursue and the environments in which you thrive.

2. **Establish Boundaries:** Setting boundaries is essential for maintaining a healthy work-life alignment. Decide how many hours you want to work each week, when you're available for meetings, and how much time you'll dedicate to personal pursuits. Clear boundaries prevent burnout and ensure that your work aligns with your overall lifestyle goals. Communicate your boundaries to employers, clients, and colleagues to foster respect and understanding. Then stick to your boundaries! If this is hard for you, consider finding an accountability partner to help you hold your boundaries, or create consequences for yourself (or others) if your boundaries are crossed.

3. **Create a Personal Income Strategy:** Develop a comprehensive income strategy that includes short-term and long-term goals. Consider diversifying your income streams to reduce reliance on a single source. Outline steps to achieve your goals, such as saving a certain percentage of your income, investing in assets, or starting a side business. Then implement one small step each week towards each of those goals. Regularly review and adjust your strategy to stay on track and adapt to changing circumstances.

4. **Embrace Work-Life Integration:** Rather than striving for a perfect balance between work and life, consider integrating the two. This means blending your professional and personal activities in a way that enhances your overall quality of life. For instance, if you enjoy traveling, look for remote work opportunities that allow you to explore new places

while earning an income. By designing your income around your lifestyle, you create a more fulfilling and sustainable way of living.

As Dan Sullivan says, "Set your own rules so you aren't following others'."

It took me a while to figure out my own rules of engagement—and the ones I wanted to encourage my clients to have. After five years of doing "financial plans" for people, I had a crisis of confidence. Every time I handed out a nicely bound, beautifully graphed plan, I had a horrible feeling in my gut.

Financial plans are mathematically correct, yet they often have nothing to do with people's lives. Think about the questions they start with: When do you want to retire? What income do you want to have? What happens if you die? Nobody knows the answers to these questions! Yet a numerical answer gets put into the software, a whole bunch of assumptions get made, and an answer gets spit out that families use to make decisions. This is scary!

Since I didn't want to keep doing those plans, I started asking financially successful people from the bank, life insurance, and mutual fund connections, "What are you doing?"

The answers all boiled down to the following, which I call the 7 Phases of Perpetual Wealth:

1. Start where you are (not where you think you want to be).
2. Measure backwards about the progress you have made (don't try to figure out forwards).
3. Develop a Prosperity mindset habit (not a fear-based, scarcity one).
4. Protect and Build at the same time (instead of saving for some day).
5. Make wealth about cash and cash flow (instead of focusing

on net worth).

6. Remember legacy is what we leave in our families (not to them).
7. Keep growing and giving (and don't retire).

When considering the rules of engagement and 7 Phases of Perpetual Wealth above, I encourage you to consider starting with the simple act of saving money when it comes to intentional income design. The Maximum Potential calculator examples in the next section from my husband Todd Langford of TruthConcepts.com prove you can build millions by simply saving, putting a bit more aside every year in a boring yet efficient way (like cash value life insurance and/or just a savings account). This is an alternative strategy we recommend rather than following the typical "swing for the fences" approach to making millions, which tends to rollercoaster people's money (and consequently their brains, feelings, confidence levels, etc.).

Maximum Potential Calculator

Okay, so let's look out over 35 years (*years* to illustrate) in the Truth Concepts calculator graphics on the following 12 pages.

Current age 35, no current assets, annual income, $100,000 a year (could be a person or a family). We see three and a half million dollars cumulative over that timeframe.

Figure 1

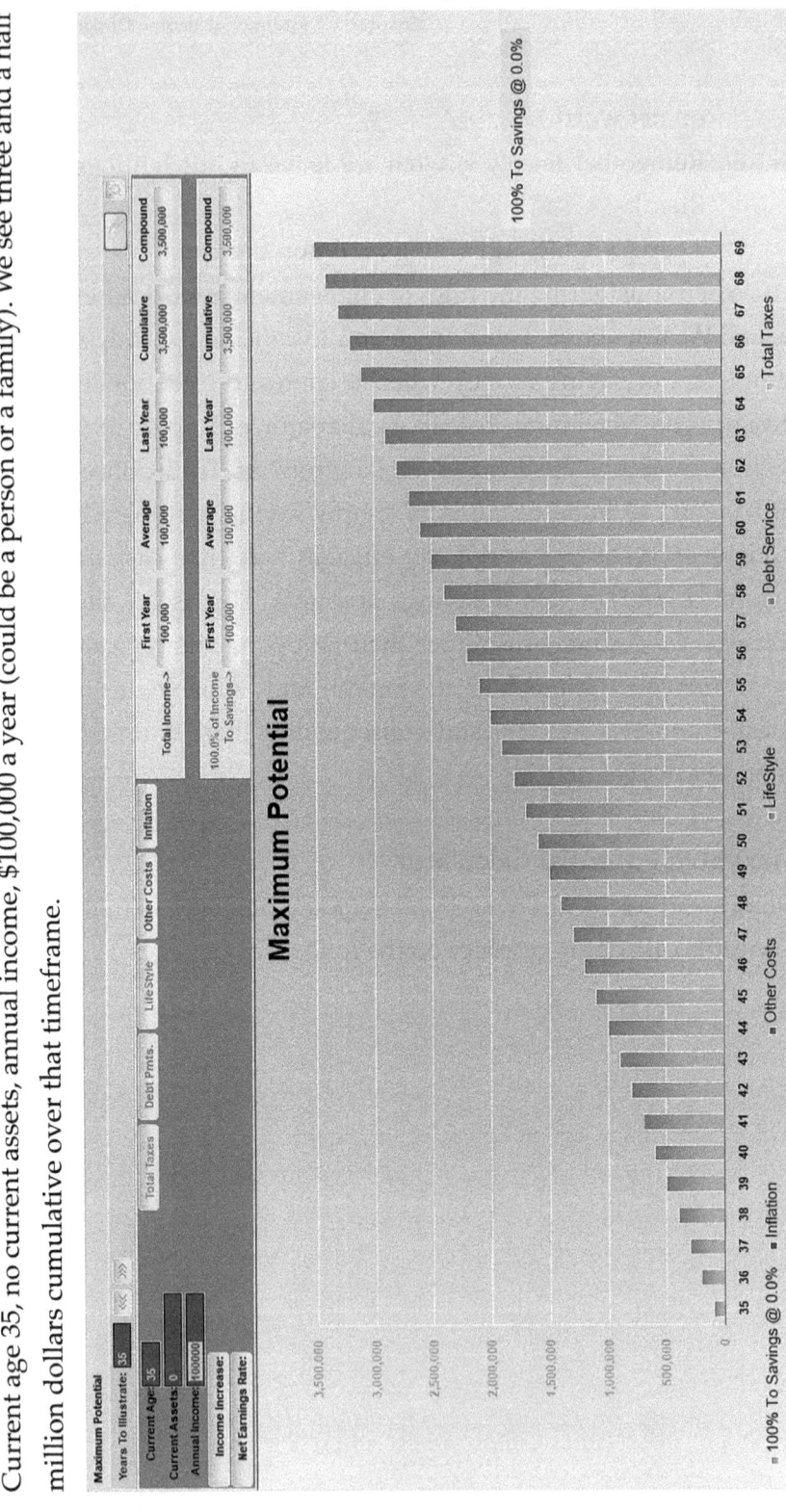

Add in the cost of living increase under the income increase box at 4%, then we see that actually cumulatively with that increase 4% every year, we would end up with a little over $7.3 million.

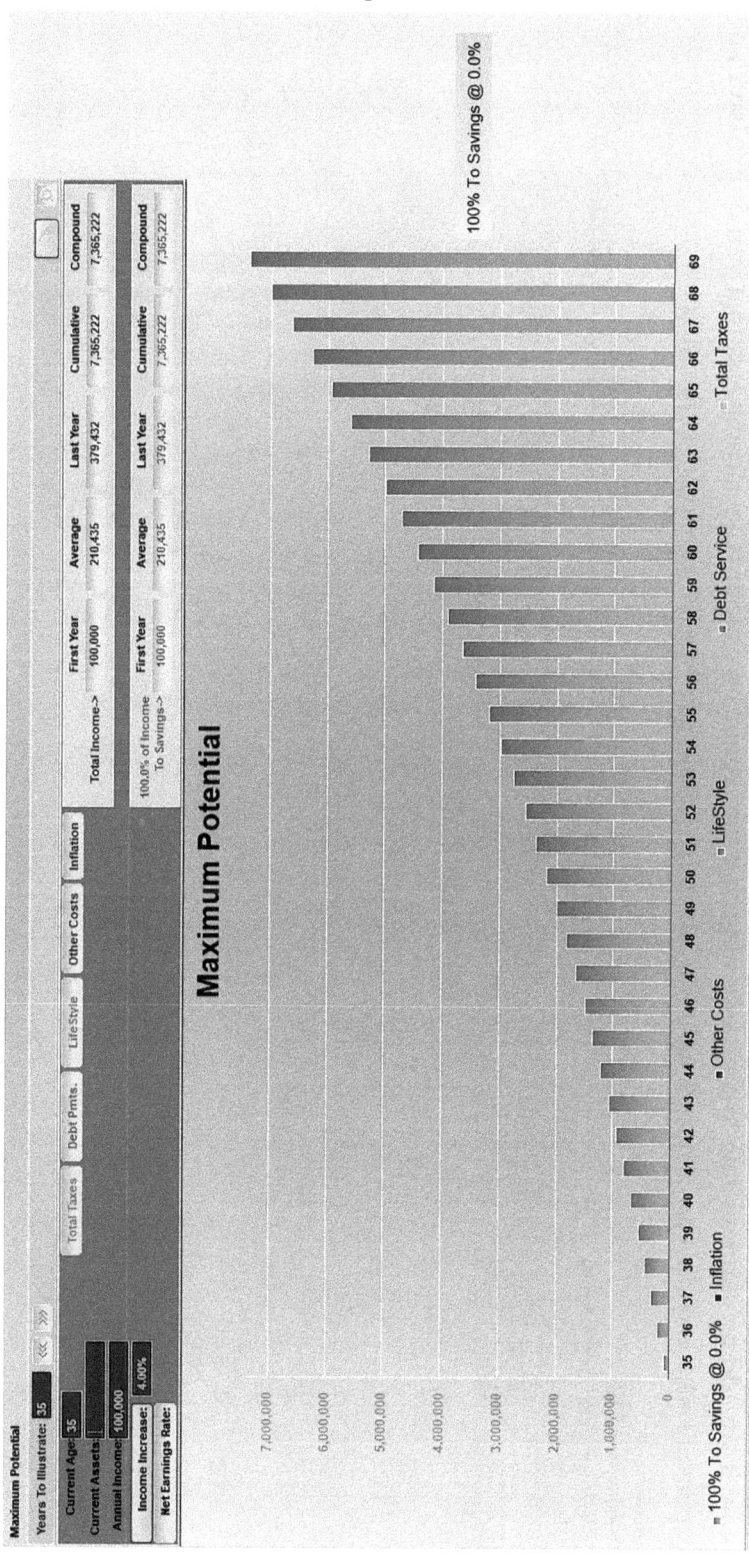

Figure 2

Now if we add an earnings rate to this, assuming that you could save all of your income and that you didn't have any expenses and you could earn a net 4% after fees, then that would grow to 13.8 million over that timeframe.

Figure 3

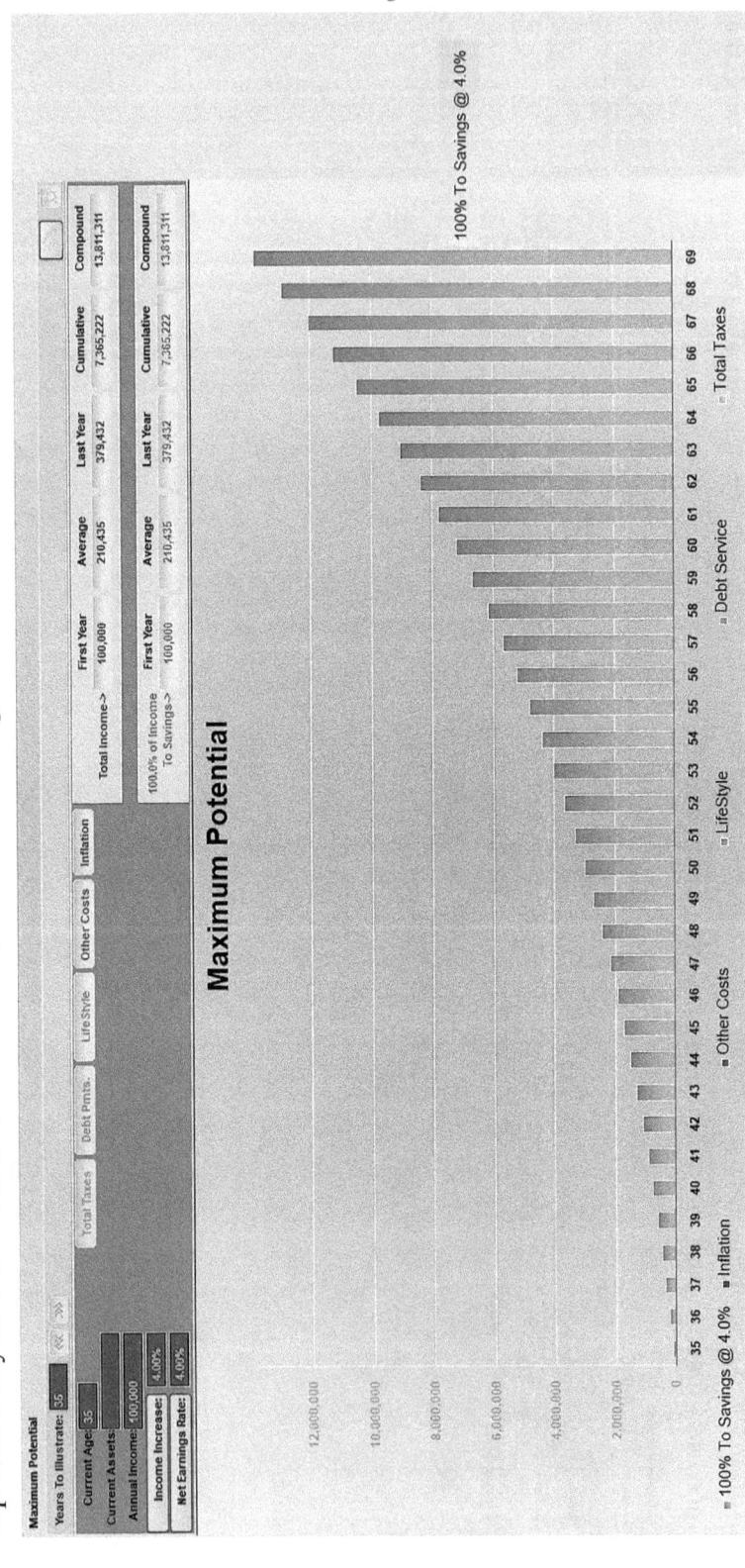

And we know we can't do that because we have things that are getting in the way like taxes. So we go to Total Taxes and we put 35% of our income into taxes, including federal, state, sales tax, property tax, etc. Then we see $2.5 million cumulatively for tax, yet that actually reduced our future from $13.8 million down to $8.9 million, which is a loss of $4.8 million. So while the taxes were only $2.5 million, our account was reduced by $4.8 million because we pay our taxes along the way, which reduces the amount of money working on earning interest in the account. This is known as opportunity cost.

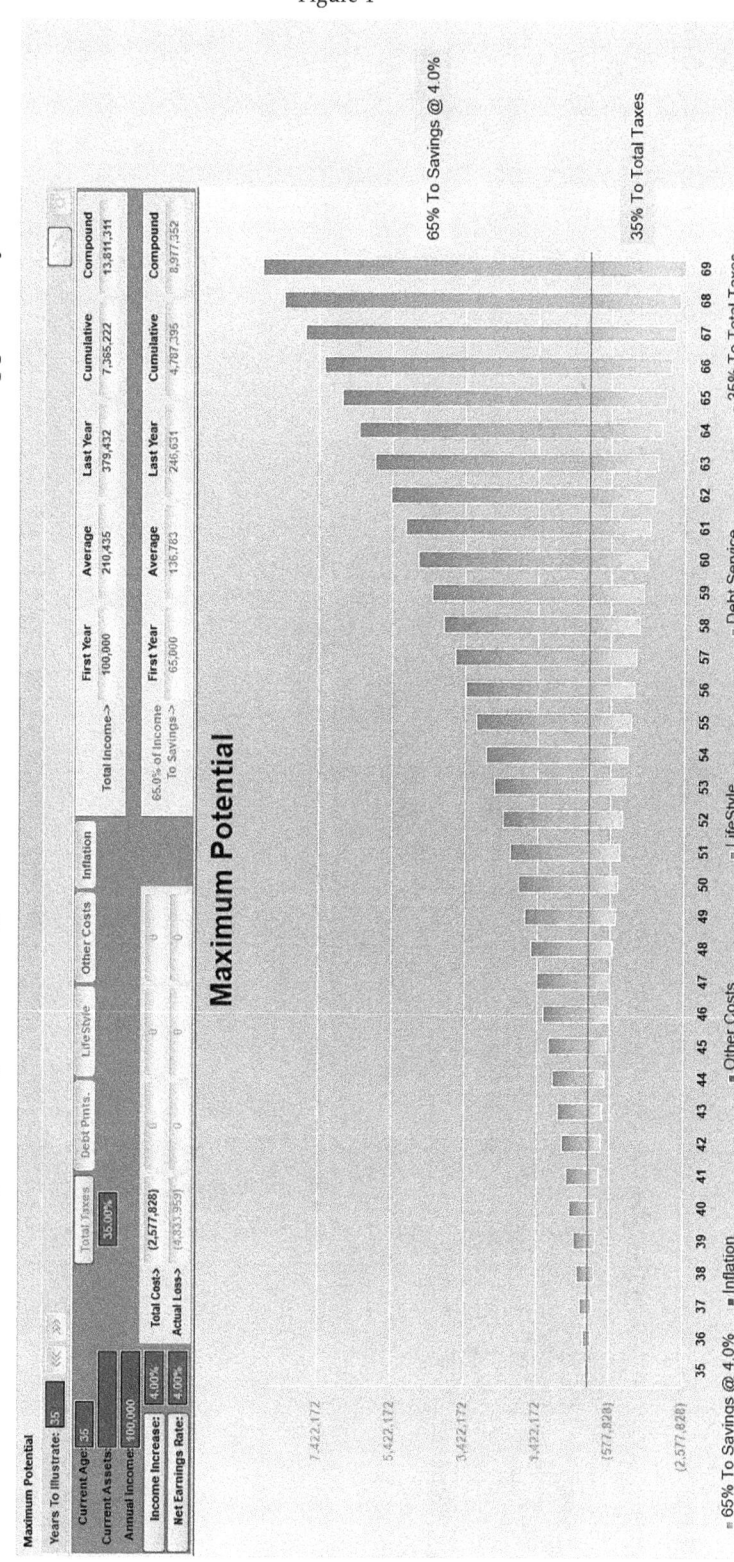

Figure 4

If we add debt payments of 30%, then we see $2.2 million in cumulative cost, that equates to $4 million of loss in future assets, again due to opportunity cost.

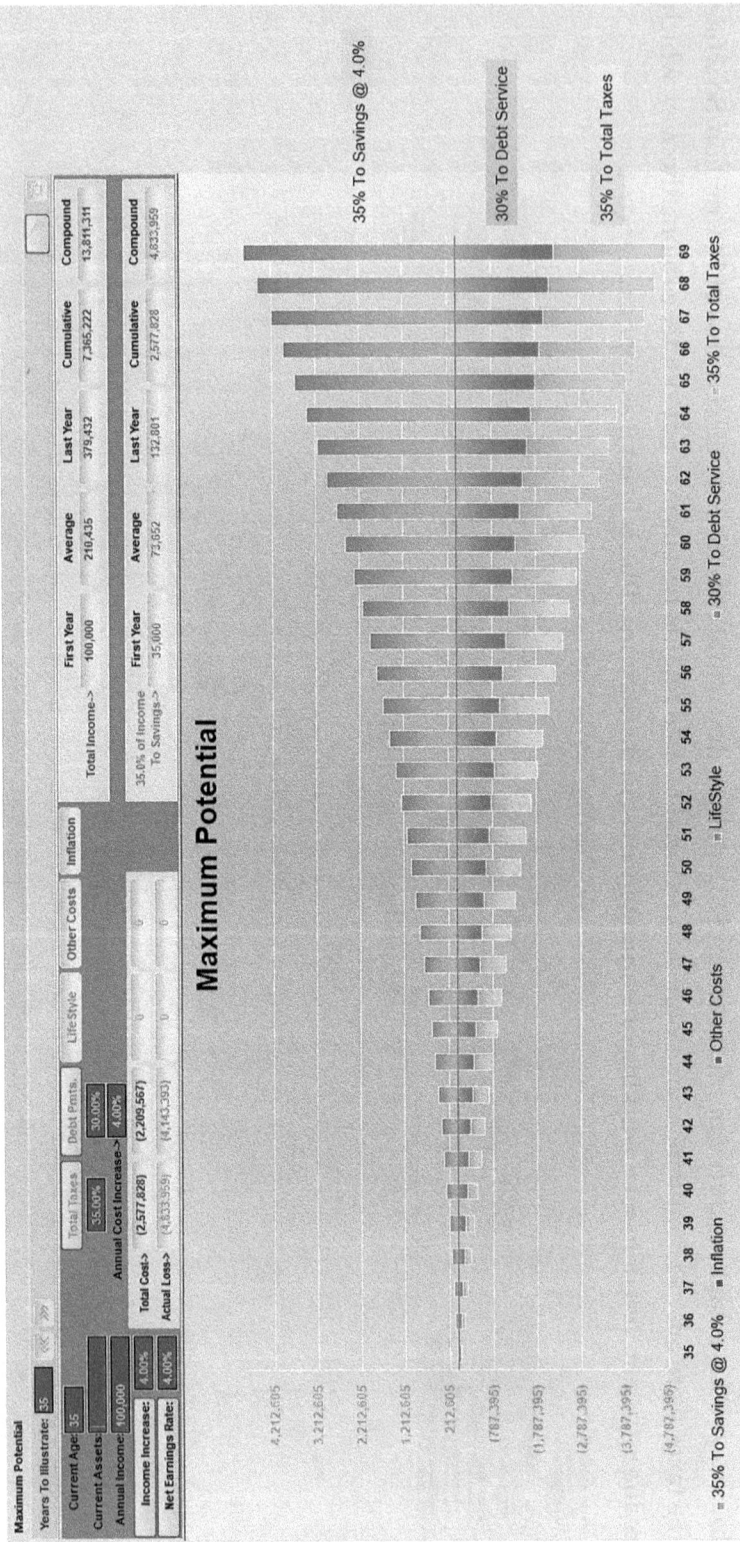

Figure 5

Figure 6

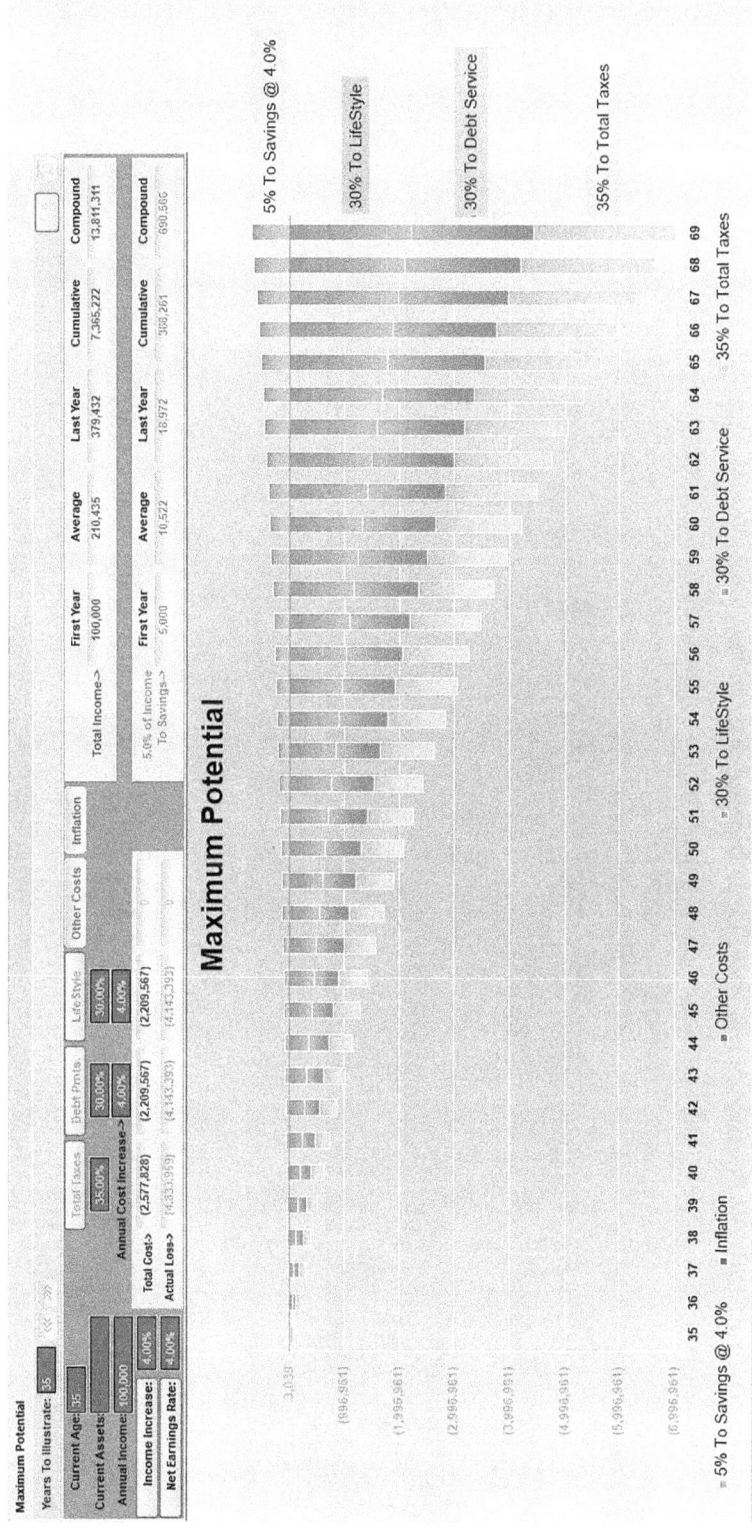

And then lifestyle at 30% gives us the same $2.2 million cumulatively taken out for a $4.1 million loss in future assets. And that whittled that $13.8 million down to $690,000.

If we look at the $690,000, because of our increase in income over those years, it's only going to give us 2.9 years of income. So we end up with that $690,000, but because we're pulling out income at that point in time, it only lasts about three years.

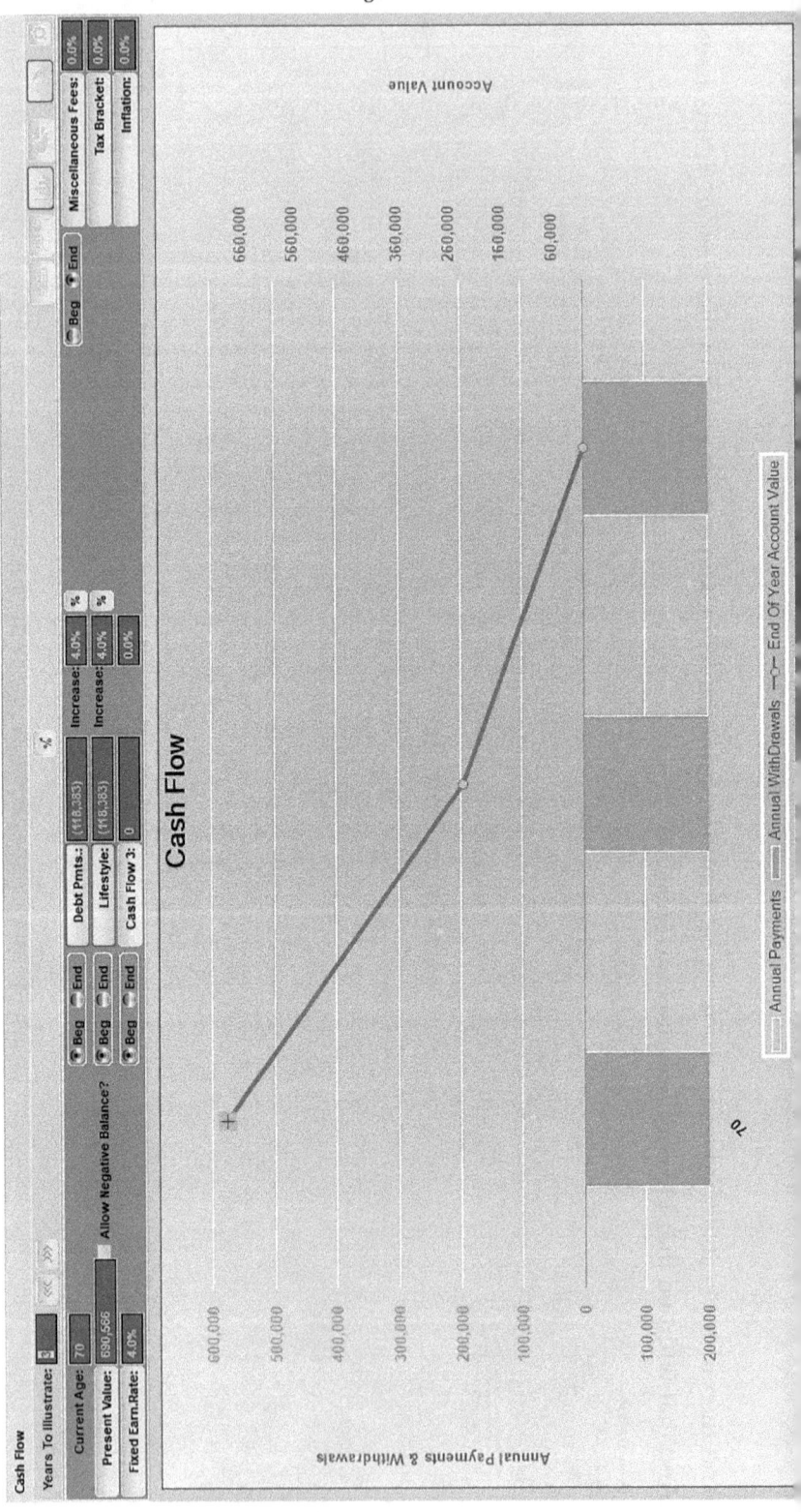

Figure 7

Now let's look at what the financial industry says we need to do to fix this. What they want to do is try to increase the earnings rate. So if we change that earnings rate to 10%, that would be 10% net of fees, we're talking about a pretty hefty return, lots of risk, and we would have to do that every single year for 35 years without any downturn. And what that would do is push us up to $2.2 million, which gives us 12.7 years of income.

Figure 8

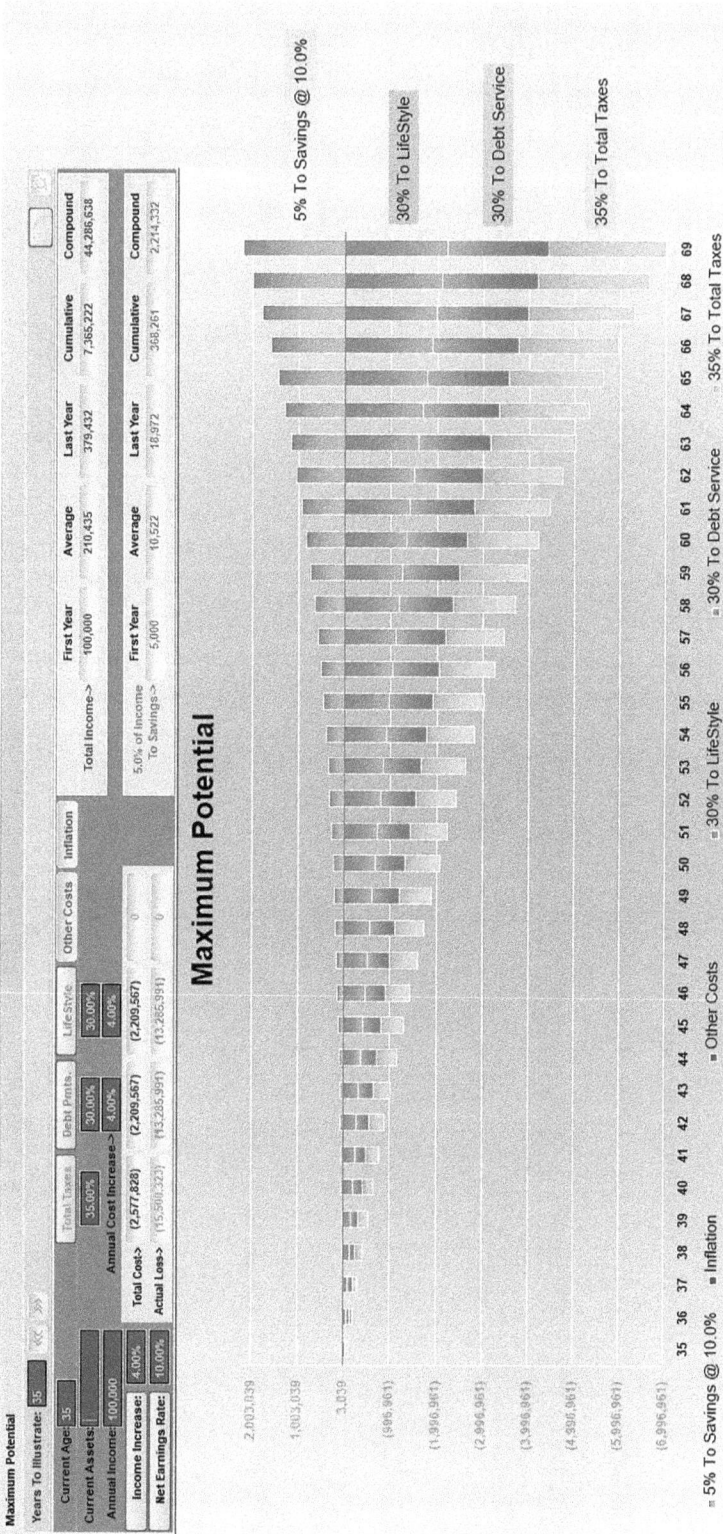

Figure 9

So it doesn't solve the problem. We have $2.2 million and we run out at age 82.

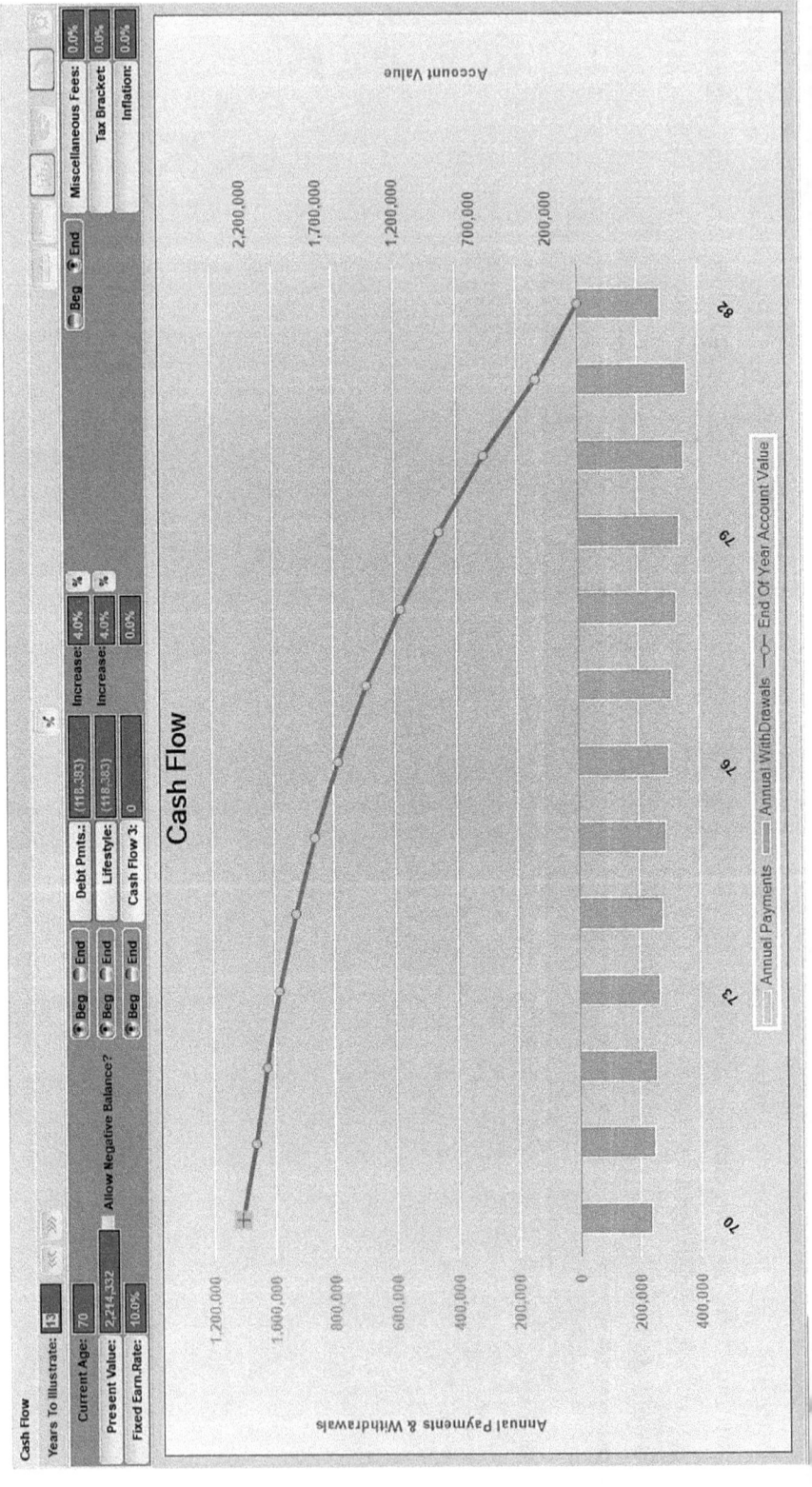

Figure 10

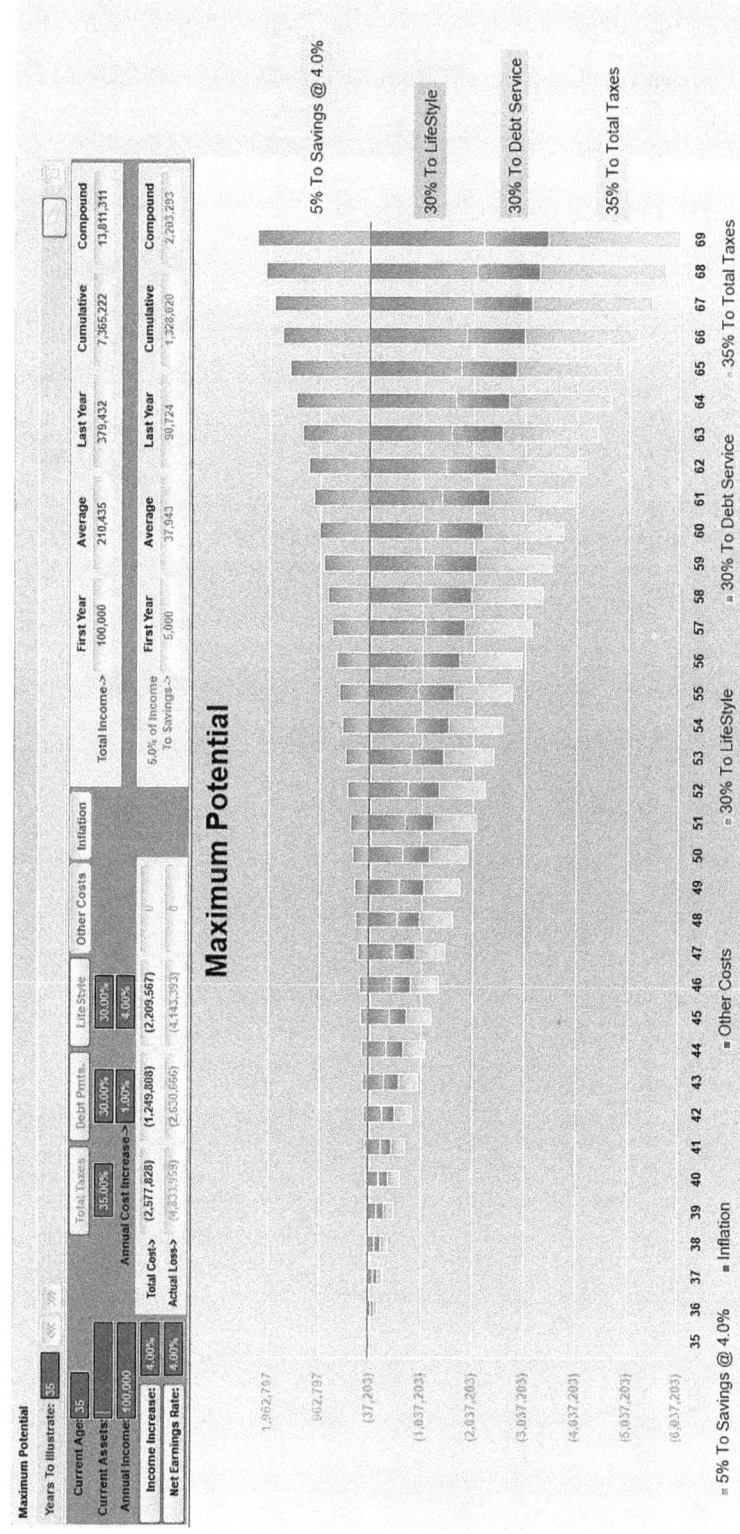

Let's look at a better option. Let's take the Earning Rate back down to something more reasonable, like 4% net of taxes. And what if we get a handle on our debt? And rather than increasing the debt amount equal to what our income is increasing, we actually reduce that increase rate. And let's say that we only increase our debt by 1% a year rather than the 4% that our income's going up.

That pushes us up to $2.2 million. And that actually moves us up to 14 years of income. And if we take this next step, we also reduce lifestyle increases, not reduce lifestyle, but just slow the increase to 2%. So we still increase lifestyle some, but at the 2% level, instead of at the 4% level.

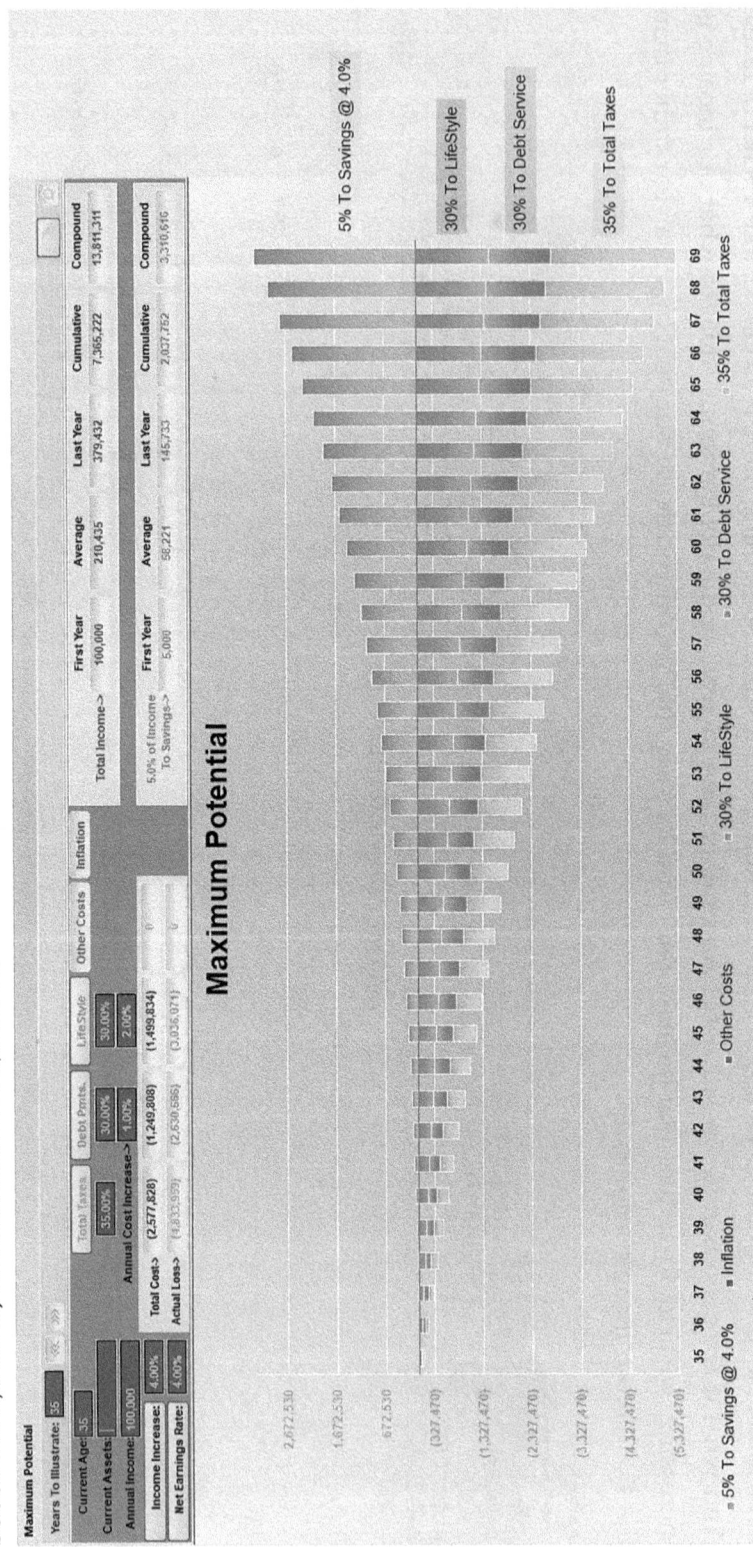

Figure 11

Figure 12

And now then that moves us to 3.3 million, which is 58 years worth of income. And let's see what that looks like. That pushes us out to age 127.

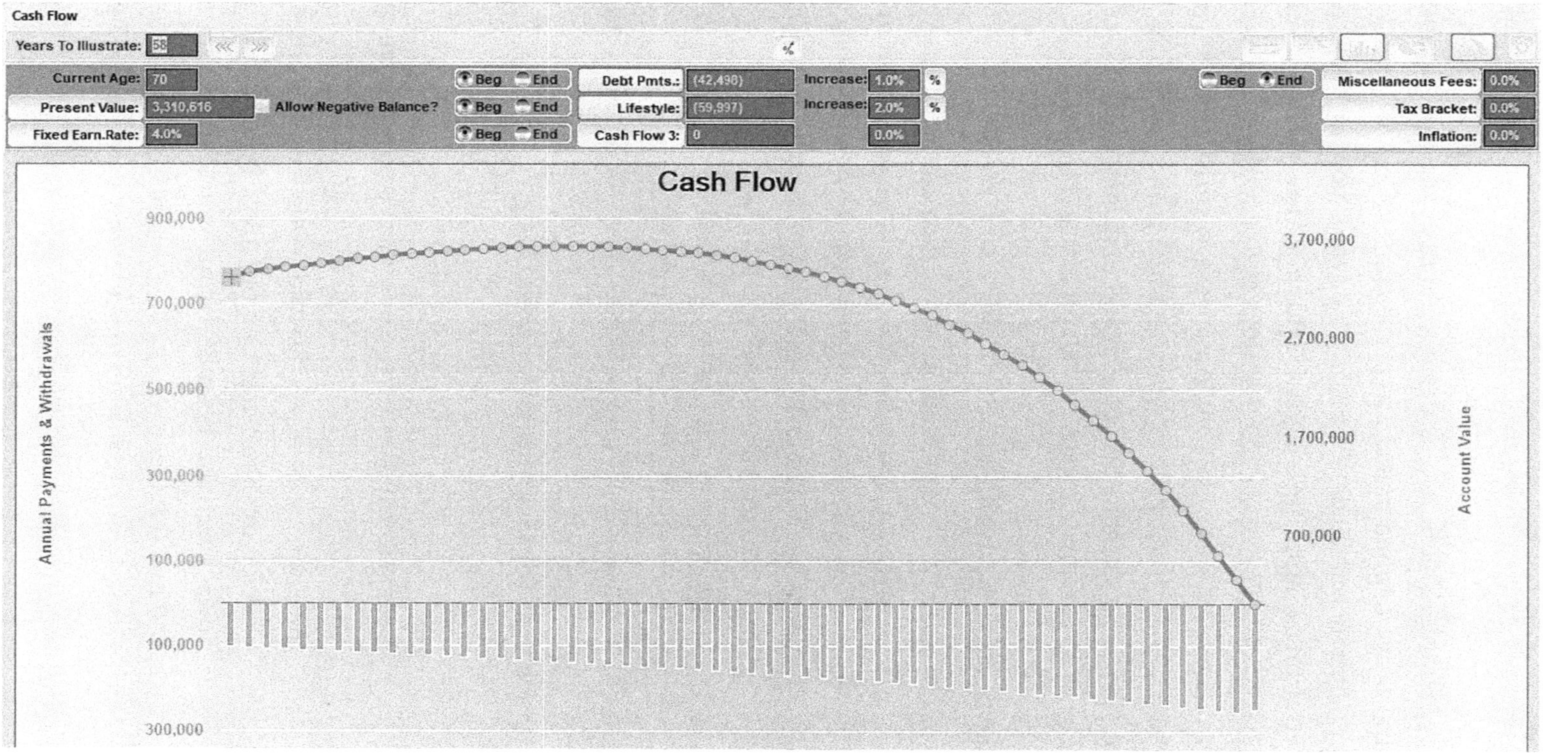

Simple. Thank you, Currence, the structure that actually makes the above happen in real life!

Intentional income design empowers you to take control of your financial future, calculate and work towards your maximum potential, and create a life that reflects your values and aspirations. By exploring various ways to increase your income, actively seek out opportunities, and set your own rules of engagement, you can achieve greater financial freedom and personal satisfaction. Remember, the key is to be proactive, adaptable, and true to yourself.

Questions for Reflection

- How can you intentionally increase your income and uncover opportunities you may not have seen before?
- In what ways have you been in default mode when it comes to income? What new ideas do you have for designing your income in the next year?
- What opportunities have you had in the past six months that you could return to for further mining?
- What are your rules of engagement for income design?

Quick Tips for Intentional Income Design

- **Be persistent. Keep looking. Keep trying.** Even if that means you're changing jobs, that's okay.
- **Keep a journal and write out what you want** over and over again each morning. You will fine-tune your intention each time you write it out. Sit and listen first to Father Mother God, or the universe, or your own intuition. Then write down what you hear. Still your mind, sit for ten minutes, and just listen.
- **Design your free time to seek your next step to find work**

that you love. We were put on Earth to serve. We give and receive, but there must be a balance. There are twenty-four hours in a day; we typically sleep eight hours, work eight hours, eat and take transportation four hours, which leaves us four free hours! What are you doing during those extra four hours? The average person watches three hours of Netflix a day! What else could you be doing with that time?

- **Take the Kolbe profile** to learn more about your modus operandi and how you work best. This will help you determine your next move for work or business, as well as how to work harmoniously with others. It's also my favorite marriage tool.
- **Let yourself fail.** This may sound counterintuitive, but we often learn our most valuable lessons by trying and failing. If a job is not for you, it's okay. Stay until you find the next one. Use the four extra hours at night to find your next job, or do the schooling or certification to better yourself, or start a business. Intentional income design is an iterative process.

CHAPTER 6

Invest in Your Growth

"An investment in knowledge pays the best interest."

BENJAMIN FRANKLIN

What do you do to invest in yourself and your growth? We've learned it's important to invest in your own growth *first*, before investing in anything else. It lays the foundation for all other forms of investment—personal, professional, or financial. When you invest your time, money and energy into your own growth, you enhance your skills, knowledge, and mindset. All of these increase your capacity to make better informed and strategic decisions.

This self-improvement not only boosts your confidence but also equips you with the tools to navigate opportunities and challenges. By focusing on your growth first, you create a strong, resilient base that supports more abundant, aligned investments in other areas of your life.

In addition, personal growth fosters an abundance mindset, which is essential for recognizing and seizing opportunities that others might overlook. This mindset shift from scarcity to abundance transforms your approach to risk and reward, allowing you to take calculated risks with a greater likelihood of success.

Investing in yourself first ensures that you are:
- Better prepared
- More adaptable
- More resilient

All of these qualities enhance your ability to invest wisely in relationships, businesses, and financial ventures. Ultimately, by prioritizing your growth, you maximize your potential and set yourself up for long-term success and fulfillment.

Investing in your growth propels you forward in all areas of life. At its core, this growth mindset opposes the scarcity mentality characterized by fear and limitation. By nurturing an abundance mindset, you can unlock greater potential, build confidence, celebrate achievements, and find joy in your work. This chapter explores three essential ways you can invest in your growth: improve yourself and build confidence, celebrate small victories, and pursue work you enjoy for lifelong growth.

Improve Yourself and Build Confidence

The journey of self-improvement begins with recognizing and nurturing your inherent strengths and capabilities. What strengths do you possess that you know you can build upon? Investing in your personal development can take many forms, such as:
- Acquiring new skills,
- Seeking mentorship, or
- Engaging in continuous learning.

Each step forward, no matter how small, helps build confidence. When you believe in your capacity for growth, you begin to see opportunities where before you saw obstacles. For example, if you feel discouraged because you don't know how to use a new technology tool in your business, you could see it as a chance to learn something new. Hop on YouTube and watch a how-to video. Or ask a friend who is proficient in the tool to teach you. When you overcome challenges and prove to yourself and others that you can do something, it naturally builds confidence.

A few easy things you can do right away to make progress on improving yourself are to:

- **Set SMART goals in areas you want to grow**: SMART stands for Specific, Measurable, Actionable, Realistic and Time-bound. Establish clear, achievable objectives to guide your growth. The more specific you are, the more specific your results will be.
- **Seek feedback**: Regularly ask people you trust and respect for constructive feedback to understand your strengths and areas you can improve. Share what you are doing and ask for their input and suggestions.
- **Reflect on your progress**: Take time to reflect on your journey, acknowledging the progress you've made. Celebrate the small wins! Look for more on this in the next section….

It's also important while working on self-improvement to practice self-compassion. Treat yourself with kindness and understanding as you would a close friend, especially in the face of setbacks. Acknowledge your efforts and progress, and avoid harsh self-criticism. This compassionate approach fosters a positive self-image and enhances your confidence. Many of us are our own worst critic, and it's good to remember that the words we say to ourselves on a daily basis matter even more than what we say to others because they form our character.

"Don't wait until everything is just right. It will never be perfect .... Get started now. With each step you take, you will grow stronger and stronger, more and more skilled, more and more self-confident, and more and more successful." —Mark Victor Hansen, author

This quote reminds me of the story from Exodus 16 in the Bible where, as the hymn says, "Day by day the manna fell." With the simplest gesture or step you take, even if it involves faith in the unseen, you gain skills and confidence that you will receive what you need.

Investing in your growth and yourself as a human being is one of the highest return investments you can make. It affects everything in your life. When you become a better human you get better business contracts, relationships, etc. Many times investing in your growth means getting help. This means being humble, coachable, and raising your hand to say, "I need help in this area."

A long time ago, I learned about Strategic Coach, and I was very clear that I wanted to invest in myself and put myself in a community of entrepreneurs who were also investing in themselves. Rather than surrounding myself with people who were limited in their thinking, these people were abundant in their thinking. Even in the face of hard challenges, the people in Strategic Coach have an abundance mindset.

For most of us, the biggest returns we've received were from many small investments in ourselves. In my life there was no big investment that caused a huge jump. Instead it was small investments over time in my growth that have created an amazing life. That includes investing in a happy life! I truly believe that the moment we stop growing we die. There's no such thing as "maintaining" a life.

For example, I worked out with a weight trainer for a long time. I had two kids, and she helped me lose weight and get a stronger body. I told her I would stop working with her and just maintain for a year, but I didn't. I ended up going back to her and asking her to help me grow again in the area of muscle strength.

Just like at the gym where we need a variety of weightlifting and exercises, we need to be active and growing in every area of our lives. I believe if you don't have a little bit of a "mid-life crisis" every ten years or so, then you're asleep at the wheel. What those crises cause is a wake-up call in us. Investing in growth when you hit a crisis like that—putting yourself in a new community, taking a class, building new relationships—is key.

I know people who, as they age, take initiative to build a new relationship with a new young person each year. Getting to experience life through others' lives is a way to invest in your growth. Enable yourself to see life through a younger set of eyes who looks at the world very differently. Young people today are very oriented towards technology, and to keep up with the advancements, committing time to a relationship with someone who is naturally attuned to that is key. We can watch, read, listen, or do whatever our favorite mode of learning is together. This is investing in our growth.

When you feel confident, you're more likely to take risks, try new things, and step out of your comfort zone. These actions can lead to significant personal and professional growth. Conversely, a scarcity mindset keeps you rooted in fear, discouraging you from seizing opportunities. Therefore, investing time and effort in self-improvement is not just about acquiring new skills but also about reinforcing your belief in your potential and planting the seeds for future opportunities.

Celebrate the Small Victories: Focus on Gains

In the pursuit of growth, it is crucial to acknowledge and celebrate small victories. These seemingly minor achievements are the building blocks of larger success. They are critical for maintaining motivation and a positive outlook.

Dan Sullivan, founder of Strategic Coach, writes about this concept with Benjamin Hardy in their book, *The Gap and the Gain*. When we measure ourselves against our ideal, we are in "the gap" mindset. However, when we measure our current success against our past selves and see how far we have come, we're in "the gain" mindset.

> *"If you focus on what you lack, you lose what you have. If you focus on what you have, you gain what you lack."* —Dan Sullivan & Benjamin Hardy, *The Gap and The Gain*

I first learned the concept of "the gap" and "the gain" from my soccer coach at Principia College. Below is an excerpt from my story as it's written in *The Gap and The Gain* that highlights how I applied the lessons I learned from my soccer coach to my career in personal finance:

> *"Ten years later, Kim became a successful entrepreneur, running a financial advising firm. When she learned about the GAP, she realized she had stopped practicing the principle her soccer coach had taught her, which was crucial to her team's success.*
>
> *As a young entrepreneur, Kim had developed the bad habit of measuring herself against her continually growing ideals.*
>
> *She realized why she wasn't as happy and successful as she could be. She wasn't measuring herself backward.*

She'd been in the GAP for years.

She started measuring herself backward, in the GAIN, and immediately she became happier, more confident, and more successful.

She now bases her entire approach to financial advising on a GAIN perspective.

Rather than helping her clients focus on a budget or their net worth, both of which are forward measures, she helps them focus on how much they have saved and how much income they are making off their investments, both of which are backward measures.

Kim asks these questions:

- *Over the past 90 days, how much money have you saved, which you now have in case of emergency or opportunity?*
- *Over the past 90 days, how much income have you earned from your investments?*

That's measuring backward.

That's focusing on what is actually tangible, and continually increasing your tangible measurables.

Like everyone, Kim still goes into the GAP. But she lets herself go there for only 5 minutes. Then, once the 5 minutes are up, she goes straight into the GAIN.

Only when you're in the GAIN can you move forward.

Being in the GAIN is how you take responsibility for your life and outcomes. You accept where you are, dust yourself off, and move forward with a smile."

Recognizing your progress, no matter how incremental, helps shift your focus from what you lack (a hallmark of a scarcity mindset) to what you have gained (a sign of an abundance mindset).

Three easy ways you can get into a gain mentality and celebrate your victories are to:

- **Acknowledge Your Achievements**: Recognize and celebrate your accomplishments, no matter how small. Start a "gains" journal in which you enter your top three gains for that day each night before going to bed.
- **Reward Yourself**: Treat yourself for reaching milestones to maintain motivation. What do you feel most rewarded by?
- **Share Your Successes**: Discuss your progress with others to reinforce your achievements. When we highlight our past achievements, we verbally affirm what we are capable of and create a foundation with our words for our next achievement.

These acknowledgements and rewards serve as reminders of your progress and the efforts you've invested. They help you maintain a positive attitude, which is essential for sustained growth and development.

Focusing on gains rather than gaps transforms how you perceive challenges and setbacks. Instead of seeing them as failures, you start viewing them as learning experiences and stepping stones to further growth. This shift in perspective is powerful. It enables you to maintain momentum and continue investing in your growth with a sense of optimism and resilience.

Pursue Work You Enjoy for Lifetime Growth

Are you currently doing work you love that you can foresee yourself doing for years to come? Finding and pursuing work that you genuinely enjoy is a cornerstone of long-term growth and fulfillment. When you engage in work that resonates with your passions and interests, you are more likely to experience a sense of purpose and satisfaction (as previously discussed in Chapter 4). This intrinsic motivation drives you to excel and continuously improve, fostering both personal and professional development.

Unsure how to discover work you enjoy or how to know if you're in it now? Try these three tips:
- **Identify Your Passions**: Discover what truly excites and motivates you in your work. Take a quiz like Kolbe or How to Fascinate to gain insights, whether you are completely at a loss for what lights you up, or whether you know and simply want a fresh perspective.
- **Seek Aligned Opportunities**: Look for people, job roles and projects that align with your interests and strengths. Volunteer or offer to help to get your foot in the door, then notice how the opportunities expand from there.
- **Stay Adaptable**: Embrace change and be open to new experiences that can further your growth. Acknowledge that change is the only constant, and to grow, you must always be adapting.

An abundance mindset plays a vital role in this self-growth process. It encourages you to seek opportunities aligned with your passions rather than settling for jobs that merely fulfill basic needs. Believing in the abundance of opportunities allows you to take bold steps toward a career that brings joy and fulfillment, which in turn, fuels your growth.

If you're still unclear about what work you feel most passionate about and need a clearer sense of direction, reach out to Tammi Brannan at BlueprintProcess.com. Additionally, there are two excellent books I recommend below. These are great for reflecting on other people's stories in order to gain greater clarity and insight for your own:
- *What Should I Do With My Life?* by Po Bronson
- *The Great Work of Your Life: A Guide for the Journey to Your True Calling* by Stephen Cope

Both of these books help elucidate the experiences of others in order to guide you in uncovering your truest work. This concept of true work, purpose, or dharma, goes beyond our culture's limited notion of a job. It is more about the overall reason you are here and what gifts and talents you feel compelled to share. When you identify these, God, or the universe, begins to line up people and resources in your favor to help you do what you are here to do.

Pursuing enjoyable work means staying open to new experiences and being willing to adapt and evolve. The world of work is constantly changing in this information age, and those who embrace an abundance mindset are more likely to thrive. They see change as an opportunity for growth rather than a threat. This adaptability ensures that you continue to grow and develop throughout your career, finding new ways to leverage your strengths and passions. It also helps you feel free to pivot when you feel you've outgrown a position or find yourself more interested or passionate about a different business or industry.

A very important part of investing in yourself, especially when you find work you enjoy, is turning around and investing that knowledge back into the world so others can learn from it as well. Teaching and mentoring is such an important part of learning. See one, do one, teach one. This is a teaching method that will naturally cause growth for both the teacher and the student. Not only do you have to grow to learn something mentally, you have to put it into play, and then you have to know it even better to teach or coach what you've learned.

And if you're humble, you can learn from your students. It brings in humble confidence. I've been in Strategic Coach thirty years because of the attitude of humble confidence that the bulk of Strategic Coach participants have. We're all there as confident entrepreneurs, yet we're all coachable.

Investing in your growth is an ongoing journey that requires a mindset shift from scarcity to abundance. By improving yourself and building confidence, celebrating small victories, and pursuing work you enjoy, you create a fulfilling and growth-oriented life. Embrace the abundance mindset, believe in the endless possibilities before you, and watch as your personal and professional life flourishes.

Questions for Reflection

- What do you do to invest in yourself and your growth now?
- What have you done recently that boosted your confidence?
- What are three small wins or gains you had in the past week?
- How have you seen your work evolve over your career so far?
- What is your "dream job" and who do you know who does something similar who you can take to lunch?

Quick Tips for Investing in Your Growth

- **Take the Gallup CliftonStrengths assessment** to discover your five top strengths. Learn how to invest in those strengths and develop skills that will help you grow in your work, financial knowledge, and relationships.
- **Purchase items as investments that help you learn the way you learn best.** They could include books, videos, courses, in-person classes, retreats, etc. It's important that you tune inward to your own intuition and pay attention to how you learn and grow best. Which learning resources will help you take the God-given talents you were born with, put them into the marketplace to benefit others, and create growth in you?
- **"Eat the frog" first thing in the morning.** The "frog" is an

undesirable task you really don't want to do. When it comes to undesirable tasks, it is not can or can't; it is will or won't. There are times where I wouldn't normally do something, but I will do it because my energy is high. For most people, that's in the morning. Every single one of us, morning or night people, are typically fresh in the morning when we wake up. If you have something you "can't" do, do it in the morning. When we invest in ourselves, we find there are many hard things we will encounter, but we can and will do them if we time them right. And every time we do, we get stronger.

- **Find a community that will support your growth**: church, work study, book study, networking group, friends, and accountability partners are all good options. Some do better with social circles, others need quiet and nature to grow. Sometimes what serves us best is doing the thing we're not naturally inclined to do. I am a total introvert who is happy at home. Two friends is enough, but I know better than to just let that lie. So I put myself in Strategic Coach, and I attend events, so that I will create opportunities to invest in myself by serving and growing in community.

CHAPTER 7

Collaborate for Exponential Increase

> "None of us, including me, ever do great things. But we can all do small things, with great love, and together we can do something wonderful."
>
> MOTHER TERESA

In today's ever-expanding, competitive financial landscape, the old adage "two heads are better than one" has never been more relevant. It's been thrilling for me to witness firsthand how collaboration can drive remarkable growth, not only for individuals but for entire organizations.

Collaboration is about more than simply working together. True collaboration involves harnessing collective strengths to achieve an exponential increase in income and impact. By aligning our efforts, sharing knowledge, and leveraging each other's expertise, we can unlock new opportunities and reach professional heights that might seem unattainable when working alone. In short, we are better together—and our results are too!

I connected with Peter Diamandis via a Dan Sullivan and Peter

Diamandis collaboration that they put together as opposed to falling into competition. It was such a great example of 1+1 = 11! Their two communities enabled exponential growth and capacity in the world. They were two businesspeople who could've said no, we are in competition with each other. Instead they said yes.

Peter possesses a very data-driven sense of optimism. This is so important for busting scarcity thinking. So many times data is taken out of context to scare people. Peter has proven year after year that health rates are up, murder is down, and he continues to share data-driven abundance-oriented news in his newsletters. I'm so grateful for it.

My fascination with scientifically proven, communal examples of abundance started with Matt Ridley's *The Rational Optimist: How Prosperity Evolves*. Then Peter came along with his book *Abundance: The Future is Better Than You Think*. Both books are excellent resources for learning more about collaborative abundance.

In Peter's "The Abundance Blog" newsletter, he wrote in June of 2024 about Blue Zones and the impact certain communal practices had on the residents there. While interviewing author, researcher and explorer Dan Buettner, Peter discovered that two of the nine fundamentals of Blue Zone wisdom are:

1. Keep parents and grandparents close by, and
2. The importance of community and your social circle.

Why are these important to note regarding collaboration? Because Blue Zones are *areas of the world where people live longer than anywhere else*. They also live healthier lives overall than anywhere else. And collaboration and community is a major factor in their longevity. Dan says, "Who we hang out with has a huge and lasting impact on our health." I would say that applies to financial health as well as physical and mental health.

My brain has been wired to look for abundance. But there are still times in my life where I need evidence like this to lean on, to remind me why collaboration matters. It's great to have scientific information that shows us abundance is numerically provable.

Be Open and Receptive to Opportunities

Embracing the art of collaboration in our work and life begins with a mindset open to new possibilities. Many people operate by default and only see and consider opportunities that are already familiar to them. However, when we open our minds to new possibilities, people, and ways of doing things, we expand our options exponentially.

If this feels hard for you because you believe your way of doing things is working just fine, try opening your mindset in a small way to start. What's a new way you could get out of bed in the morning? A new fruit or vegetable you could add to your cart at the grocery store? A new vocabulary word you could use in a sentence today?

Open-mindedness is like a muscle; small reps over time will create muscle memory and increased strength. It is also an excellent cross-training tool; being open-minded in one area of your life will naturally open your mind in all areas. It is directly connected to learning, and as long as we are learning, we are growing—both ourselves and the value we create and provide.

Once your mindset is open, you are ready to collaborate and increase your income! Below are four key ways to cultivate receptiveness to new opportunities.

- **Engage Actively:** Get more involved. Attend events, webinars, and networking functions to meet potential partners and explore collaborative opportunities. Engaging with a broader network can uncover hidden opportunities and partnerships that drive growth. During this process, be sure to focus on what you can give and offer, rather than what you can get. This will ensure you are approaching new people and opportunities with an abundance mindset rather than a scarcity one.

- **Trade Knowledge:** Be willing to offer insights and resources. This often encourages others to reciprocate, fostering a collaborative environment. Sharing expertise not only aids others but also builds a foundation of mutual support and trust. People like to work with others they know, like, and trust.
- **Soak Up Feedback:** Actively ask for feedback from peers and colleagues to gain fresh perspectives. They can help you identify potential areas for joint growth. Constructive criticism can be a catalyst for improvement and collaborative success.
- **Leverage Curiosity:** Approach every interaction with an open mind and a readiness to learn. This can lead to unexpected partnerships and income-boosting opportunities. Focus on asking questions to learn more; the paths you take in conversation may surprise you! Curiosity drives innovation and helps uncover new avenues for collaboration.

Approaching collaboration with an open, abundance-oriented mindset is attractive to new partners and communicates from the start that you are open to growth. This invites a mutual flow of creativity and unconventional income-producing ideas. In this early phase of collaboration, though you don't want to restrict or limit yourself or the people you are collaborating with, it is important to have someone capturing the ideas in some form: written, recorded, etc. This way when you're ready to make decisions and take action together, you can compare all the newly generated ideas and track your progress over time.

Reframing Crises as Opportunities

We all face crises, both personally and professionally, throughout our lives. The Greek origin of the word crisis, "krisis," means "decide." Though a crisis can be daunting, it presents an opportunity for decision and moving in a new direction. When facing a financial crisis, we may feel tempted to fall back into a scarcity mindset. However, we always have the option to choose abundance.

Gratitude recenters us and brings us back to a decision point that is rooted in abundance. It shows us what we have and reframes a difficult crisis into an opportunity for growth. Plus, we are never completely alone in any crisis. Asking for help—from your higher power, your community, your family, or your colleagues—can help you make a decision from a broader, more collaborative perspective.

Here are a few tips to reframe crises and turn them into productive professional opportunities:

- **Identify the Core Issue:** Dig deep. Analyze the crisis to understand its root cause. This clarity can guide you in finding collaborators who offer complementary skills to address the problem. For instance, a financial downturn can reveal gaps in strategy. When addressed collaboratively, this can lead to stronger, more resilient business models.
- **Combine Collective Strengths:** Use the crisis as a catalyst to pool resources and expertise, leading to innovative solutions and improved income prospects. A study by McKinsey & Company found that companies that leveraged collaborative approaches during crises were better positioned for long-term success.

- **Promote Transparent Communication:** Be constructively candid. Open dialogues during crises foster trust and cooperation, creating a stronger foundation. Transparency not only resolves immediate issues but also builds enduring professional relationships. When you are transparent through a crisis, whether personal or professional, you build trust and others can relate to your experience in an open way. We all learn from witnessing each other openly navigate tough situations.
- **Adopt a Problem-Solving Mindset:** Encourage a collaborative approach to problem-solving, turning challenges into opportunities for professional growth and increased revenue. As Romans 8:28 (NIV) reminds us, "And we know that in all things God works for the good of those who love him, who have been called according to his purpose." When we are all working towards a bigger "why," a greater goal, we are motivated by something larger than ourselves. From this standpoint, we can tap into higher level collaboration and solutions.

Asking for Help: Invite Professional Partnership

Reaching out for help is not a sign of weakness; rather, it's a strategic move that can foster strong professional partnerships. Here's how asking for assistance can lead to valuable collaborations:

- **Communicate Your Needs:** What fuels you? Recognize and communicate your specific needs, which can attract partners who possess the skills and resources required to address those gaps. Being clear about what you need helps others understand how they can contribute effectively. People want to help and give. By communicating your needs clearly (in an open, curious way rather than a desperate, scarcity-minded way), you give them the opportunity to do so.

- **Build Trust:** Asking for help builds trust and demonstrates vulnerability, which can strengthen professional relationships and lead to more effective collaborations. (See my recommendation of Brené Brown's book, *Dare to Lead* below for more on this topic.) Trust is the bedrock of successful partnerships and can lead to more significant and ongoing opportunities.
- **Foster Mutual Benefit:** When you seek assistance, ensure that the collaboration benefits both parties, creating a win-win situation. Ideally, it should enhance professional growth and/or income for both parties in the long run. Mutual benefit ensures that all parties are invested in the success of the collaboration.
- **Focus on Growth:** Use requests for help as opportunities to explore new avenues for collaboration, leading to expanded networks and increased income. This approach fosters an environment of mutual support and growth. It guarantees the arrangement is not one-sided and serves a greater purpose than simply meeting one need.

Ways to Collaboratively Increase Income

Many creative routes exist that can spark exciting new ventures for collaborative income growth. The trick is determining which ones will yield the results you seek. Here are some practical channels to consider:

- **Joint Ventures:** Partner with other professionals to offer combined services or products, expanding your market

reach and revenue potential. For instance, combining financial planning with legal services can attract clients seeking comprehensive solutions.
- **Cross-Promotions:** Uplift each other's profit. Collaborate with peers to cross-promote each other's services or products, leveraging each other's networks to attract new clients. Cross-promotion can enhance visibility and lead to new business opportunities. Link to each other's websites online, share knowledge in joint email campaigns or work together on a project you can cross-promote.
- **Shared Resources:** Trade useful tools with people you trust. Pool resources such as office space, marketing budgets, or technology to reduce costs and increase profitability. Shared resources can lead to significant cost savings and more effective use of assets.
- **Innovative Projects:** Launch joint projects or initiatives that tap into new markets or address emerging needs, generating additional streams of income. Innovation often thrives in collaborative settings, leading to breakthrough ideas and new revenue streams.

Whether you are collaborating for an individual reason or a business purpose, these tips above can all apply. When you focus on *who* can help you, you realize there are an abundance of resources available to you at any given moment.

A long time ago I met Patrick Donahoe who owns Paradigm Life (and who wrote the foreword for this book). He was new in life insurance at the time. My husband and I attended a dinner with him and shared everything we could to help him, believing in the benefits of collaboration and there being enough business for all of us.

Fast forward ten years: Todd and I wanted to create a community for whole life-friendly financial advisors. We knew Patrick had a wide reach at that point and asked him to join us. He was a direct competitor, but our audience was our peers (who could've all been competitors too!). Right about that time, Patrick had an opportunity in a marketing space that funneled him more people than he could possibly help on his own. He then offered those referrals to me.

There was this huge space of giving first. Nobody was keeping score or tracking who did what. Everybody was just using the God-given talent they had to help as many people as possible. The community for advisors and the marketing opportunity played themselves out. And Todd, Patrick and I just kept giving and creating that 1+1=11 environment. I know 1+1=2, yet I like to say it equals eleven to indicate the exponential nature of collaboration and the even more expansive nature of the effect of networks.

We have since collaborated on a webinar for Patrick's clients and my clients, as well as a variety of things for Todd's business. We've helped him, and he's helped us. Everybody's staying in their lanes, but bringing our three talents together (1+1+1) has been an opportunity to see that collaboration can overtake competition any day of the week.

Patrick also introduced us to the Network Effect, and there's a whole class you can take that is a good example of how collaboration is a step above competition. I believe the Network Effect will be an even further step above collaboration. Collaboration is usually 1+1 and affects a group of people. The Network Effect takes that concept and applies it exponentially whereby not only are the leaders of the group affecting their own community, but community members are affecting community members too. If you think about a network, you get these nodes interplaying with other nodes, in turn creating their own exponential impact. The growth of the goodness going on there becomes exponentialized.

Take the First Step—Together

The Harvard Business Review reported that collaboration is crucial for innovation and business success in their article, "Why Collaboration Is Critical in Uncertain Times," underscoring the importance of collective efforts. This article reminds us, "when you need to reassess your business strategy during uncertain times, remember that the key is to view collaboration not as a nice-to-have but as an indispensable asset on your growth journey."

Collaboration isn't merely a strategy; it's a social art form and a powerful approach that can lead to exponential increases in income and professional success. By embracing openness, viewing crises as opportunities, seeking help, and diving into creative solutions, we can swim in synergies that drive remarkable growth.

The future of professional achievement and abundance lies in our ability to work together and leverage our collective strengths. When we embrace collaboration with enthusiasm and optimism, together we can achieve extraordinary results.

For additional reading and motivation on the power of collaboration and its effective impact on professional and personal success, check out the following books:

- *The Collaborative Habit: Life Lessons for Working Together* by Twyla Tharp—Offers insights into the collaborative process and how to cultivate a successful mindset in that vein.
- *Team of Teams: New Rules of Engagement for a Complex World* by General Stanley McChrystal—Explores how collaboration and adaptability can lead to extraordinary achievements.
- *Dare to Lead: Brave Work. Tough Conversations. Whole Hearts.* by Brené Brown—Shows you how to recognize the potential in people and ideas and have the courage to develop that potential.

The journey to achievable, exponential growth begins with a single step towards collaboration. Who do you know that you can reach out to today for a call or a meeting? Take that courageous step—the possibilities are boundless and bright!

Questions for Reflection
- When have you gone through a crisis that your community helped you get out of?
- Where do you find opportunities to connect and expand your impact? Where might you look that you haven't yet?
- Is asking for help easy or hard for you? If it's easy, try offering help to someone you know. If it's hard, try asking for help from someone for a simple task.
- Have you collectively/collaboratively increased your income before? Who did you partner with? What lessons did you learn?

Quick Tips for Collaborating for Exponential Increase
- **Ask the person closest to you what their values are** and write them down on a post-it or card. Keep it next to yours. When you combine your efforts with a close friend, family member, or spouse, it is like a tornado going upwards, ever growing. It's exponential, like the example of 1+1 = 11. The more common saying is 1+1 = 3, but 1+1 is visually 11 on paper. That's indicative of the exponential nature that occurs when you put two things together that have that ever-expanding, ever-increasing environment going. You get a multiplier effect instead of just an additive effect. We all know 1+1=2, but 1+1=11 emphasizes the multiplying effect we can have on each other's efforts, rather than just

an additive effect. Kristen and I co-writing this book was a great example of this principle in action.

- **Learn the love languages, Kolbe Profiles, Treasure Tree personality types, or other assessment information about the people closest to you.** Let that lead and form collaboration. Discuss it at family dinnertime or lunchtime at the workplace. When you're clear on what you bring to the table, that makes room for other people's gifts. You're self-aware of what you bring, which also makes you conscious of what you don't bring—and what you can collaborate with others on.
- **Say no more often. Have a not-to-do list.** This will help you hone in on your true strengths and find people to collaborate with who respect your boundaries. Then you will absolutely get 1+1 = 11. Don't try to be other people. Be the best *you* you can be, while at the same time still growing.
- **Collaborate with ideas, books, and spaces in addition to people.** Collaboration doesn't always have to be with individuals. When you collaborate with new ideas—through activities like brainstorming or journaling—they can give you new perspectives and connections that will increase exponentially. There is no end to ideas!
- **Incorporate younger generations in your life.** If you don't have kids, go teach Sunday School, serve at a Boys and Girls club, or interact with kids at the park or in the grocery store. Smiling and striking up a conversation is free and easy. Younger generations have fresh new perspectives. If you are in your eighties, you should have two to three generations of children below you that you are engaging with. And proximity to them matters! There was a study done of

a senior care facility next to a Kindergarten where they tore down the brick wall between them and put up a glass wall, and it was extremely valuable for both generations to see each other. In the *Stanford Social Innovation Review*, an article on "The Power of Proximity" highlights multiple studies like this on the benefits of connections and collaborations between generations.

BONUS
CHAPTER 8

Share the Love: Abundant Families and Relationships

> "We make a living by what we get,
> but we make a life by what we give."
>
> WINSTON CHURCHILL

Now that you know how to transform a scarcity mindset into a prosperity mindset, how will you share your knowledge and your wealth with the people you love? In this bonus chapter, I share specific stories and examples of how Kristen and I have shared and witnessed others sharing their abundance to spark ideas and inspiration. May the abundance of love flow through your home, your relationships, your family, your work, your hobbies, and your bank account.

Abundant Families

At one family gathering of our whole family—with four adult children, including my sister's kids, and their children—we were all talking about bringing together our individual values and creating common shared values for our family. We discussed the idea of writing them in a book, laying them out on the table, or even playing a card game that could help us with our value orientation, such as *Family Legacy* (a card game that drives values), or *The Quiet Year*, another game that creates conversations around values. It helps to have a structure in which to discuss your family values.

Free Time

One value I share with most of my family is free time together. I learned the concept of free days, focus days, and buffer days from Dan Sullivan in 1995. This powerful concept transformed my time with my children. I started working with Strategic Coach before they were born. Prior to that I had been a typical entrepreneur viewing every day as a workday. That's an a1 problem. It took me a while to rearrange my calendar and my habits to free myself up, first on Sunday, then Saturday, then on an occasional day during the week. This free time allowed me to be completely present with my kids.

In order to value and protect this free time, however, I had to purchase help. One of the first things I did was purchase bookkeeping help. Before the internet, I spent two to four hours a month balancing my checkbook, moving money around, reconciling accounts, etc. So one of the first delegations and hires I made was a bookkeeper, Carrie Putnam, who still works with me today! She took over my personal and business books. Now I could implement the ideas I was paying Strategic Coach for, such as having a free day with my family each week and protecting time with them. This required a money commitment (to hire Carrie) as well as a calendar commitment (to not let business activities creep into Saturday or Sunday).

When I walked out of my first session with Strategic Coach, I already had an assistant for my business. I knew that I could hire a part time bookkeeper and housecleaner. They both helped in huge ways to free up time and money. A housecleaner could do a much better job than I could ever do. And for a small amount of money, it freed up a Saturday for me to rejuvenate for the week. It made me a better mom, business owner, wife, and friend.

In addition, I blocked off a nine-day week each year—a weekend on each side plus a week in the middle—so I could be fully present with my family. The values I hold dear include not doing anything business-oriented when spending time with family. This is hard when three of my family members are involved in my business! I won't say there was absolutely *no* business discussion, but for the bulk of the time, the primary focus stayed on the people we were with and the activities we were doing together. The precious space that is provided because you identify and take a free day or week is priceless. Thank you to Dan Sullivan for teaching me this idea.

Protecting Your Family Values
When you are committed to a value—family time, free time, or rejuvenation to bring your best self to your loved ones—you do whatever you can to protect it. I saw what happened when I didn't stick to those values (bringing a computer or a file home from work, for example). I became worthless as a person in the space of family, and the work I did took twice as long because I couldn't truly focus on it. Oftentimes I would never even get to the work. Then I would haul the computer or file back to the office, feeling guilty that I never got it done.

I chose rightly to do the family thing, but the computer would blink at me, or the file would be a visual reminder to me that I hadn't done what I intended to. Then 10-20% of my brain was distracted by the task, and I wasn't fully committed to the people I was there with. If I allow a client meeting to get in on a buffer day, I'm not honoring what the buffer day is all about. Focus days are like game days for a professional athlete—my entire focus needs to be on the game at hand. Self-knowledge is another really important value of mine, and it is essential when honoring your time blocks and showing up for your family. You must know yourself well enough to admit when you need to make a change.

Lean Years and Green Years
Another example of how our shared family values played out is through teaching our kids about lean years (money was tight) and green years (money was flowing well). We had the opportunity to bring all of our family together for Christmastime during a green year. We chose to purchase all of the rooms in a small resort even though a few family members couldn't come and we likely wouldn't use them all. We didn't give up those rooms because we wanted our family to have the focus it really deserved without outside distractions.

Our family members had communicated they all wanted a place they could go and be together the bulk of the time, and this was our solution. It was wintertime, so we wanted to ski, spend quality time together, and enjoy meals together. Because it was a green year, and our family understood that, it was an easy check to write and a joy to spend the money so everybody got to be together.

Purposeful Conversations
What showed up as really critical about this family experience was the importance of purposeful conversations. It is so easy at a vacation time like that to just let a week fly by with no real deep conversations. Everyone is busy, especially if there are young children involved, since they require so much. Not every meal needs to have

a purposeful conversation, but it's great to have good opening lines on hand.

Over the years, I have definitely gotten some eye rolls and reluctant answers from teens during purposeful conversations, but I stuck with it because I value meaningful communication. It is another one of our shared family values. Having perseverance in purposeful conversations means the kids in their adult years have come to ask for and expect purposeful conversations. Even during our last meal, they all asked what the purposeful conversation was going to be. Specific open-ended questions where they can't answer "yes" or "no" are important. Positive focus during these purposeful conversations is another concept from Dan Sullivan we use often in our family.

- Some examples of positive questions to start purposeful conversations are:
- What's one thing you learned this past year? (great to ask on a birthday or landmark day)
- How did you create value today?
- What was the best part of your day? Or, what was the best thing that happened to you today?
- What were the top three things that happened to you this week?
- What has to happen today for you to be pleased at the end of the day?

Because Kristen shares 50/50 custody of her children with their dad, she has created a family meeting as a reset tool for them to have an intentional purposeful conversation. They've created a habit of doing a walking family meeting every other Sunday night when they walk their dog, Shep. Kristen and her kids use three simple questions during these bi-weekly family meetings:

1. What's working in your life/our family?
2. What's not working in your life/our family?
3. What's coming up for you this week and how can we support you with that?

Each family member takes a turn sharing their answers to these three questions aloud. One of them serves as the facilitator to help keep each other on track if they forget to address a question. In a more structured setting, you might consider using a timer for each person, but Kristen has found the consistent walking route they take provides key markers to help them stay on track and know when they're a third or two-thirds of the way and it's time to switch who's talking.

Having this purposeful conversation outdoors while moving seems to help the flow and allows each person to speak freely without feeling confronted or confrontational (since they are all moving in the same direction). It allows each family member to feel heard and be recognized. Often it spurs further conversations as they collaborate to solve problems one or all of them may be facing. The open communication on a consistent basis has improved their understanding and support of each other, as well as prompted critical thinking and behavioral changes that strengthen the family as a whole.

Because good communication is a primary value of Kristen's, these bi-weekly meetings serve as a foundation for their family to improve their communication and openly share what they might not otherwise. This has been a game changer for their family in terms of expressing gratitude for what's working, letting each other know what they're going through and what might be hard (or not working), and asking for help when they need it. Abundance comes in infinite forms, and one we often take for granted is that of supportive family members.

Instead of, or in addition to, Kristen's questions above, you can use any of the liberating structures developed by Henri Lipmanowicz and Keith McCandless and detailed in their book *The Surprising Power of Liberating Structures: Simple Rules to Release a Culture of Innovation* for family meetings (or any group communication, for that matter). For quick reference, see their website at liberatingstructures.com. Play around and experiment to find a structure that works best for you and your loved ones.

If you like the stories and tips above, you may enjoy joining Prosperity Parents, a program I have created to help families become abundant. In it, I teach many of Scott Donnell's methods from The Value Creation Kid. (You can go to prosperityparents.com to see this material.) While money is not everything in life, it affects everything we do, and our relationship with money definitely affects our kids. It's important as a family to find and implement common values around money, time, space, communication, and more.

Abundance in a Romantic Relationship

In his book *The Forgotten Art of Love: What Love Means and Why It Matters*, Armin A. Zadeh, MD, PhD writes, "In an ideal relationship, each partner provides a continuous, committed effort for the well-being and happiness of the other." We all want to love and be loved. It is one of the most primal human desires. Yet, providing continuous, committed effort to help a partner live their fullest, happiest life is no easy feat. Those who do it well have discovered the "key element of the art of loving," as Zadeh describes it: "prioritizing the happiness of somebody over other impulses you may have."

I am inspired when I hear stories of couples who exemplify this abundant way of loving one another. Like anything in life, it is a practice we can improve on by witnessing others who do it well and learning from them. Kristen has two friends whose wedding reception she attended this winter. They continually inspire her in the ways they prioritize each other's happiness and keep discovering abundance in their romantic relationship.

Their names are Mary Anne and Jon. They met and started their connection with a fling in Tucson back when they were both twenty-two years old. A friend of theirs had introduced them and invited them both to a party where they hit it off right away and enjoyed some passionate encounters. Mary Anne, a dancer, enjoyed hearing Jon, an actor, describe his creative wild ideas in a coffee shop—everything from writing to being a playwright to his superhero fascinations. She described him as "thin, dark-haired, and mysterious, with a raspy voice" (that he still has today). However, at that age, their romance was fleeting. Both were busy with their creative projects, and they ended up going their separate ways.

Twenty-five years later, Mary Anne was walking into a dance rehearsal at her local studio. Jon was picking up his daughter from dance. They both got that nervous, excited feeling when they saw each other again. It was October 2013. They started talking and flirting a bit, and then Mary Anne took a chance and invited Jon to her 50th birthday party (also her annual holiday party). Ever since then they have been spending time together, prioritizing each other's happiness. They moved a bit cautiously at first and then jumped all-in. They married in December of 2024.

Both have grown adult children finding their way in the world, both have aging parents they spend hours every week caring for, and both have work and ongoing artistic pursuits—all of which pull at their time and energy. Yet they prioritize time with each other and lift each other up every chance they get. To paraphrase Maya Angelou, they are the "rainbow in each other's cloud."

To get a sense of their abundant love for one another, they've shared excerpts from their vows:

Jon

I love how we eclipse each other. I want that, forever and a day. I admire the way you find so much joy in life. I tend to look for the extraordinary, but you celebrate the extraordinary and find even the ordinary extraordinary. Every bent stick on the trail becomes a smiley face of a different kind. Every color a new hue. Every sunset or moon as if it's the first. That astounds me.

I love that you trooped through crazy backpacking trips with me without ever doing it before. When we were at the edge of the world on Catalina Island looking out over rocks with crashing waves of infinite ocean pounding them, we looked up the mountain beside us. It was supposed to have a trail to the top for an overlook, but we found no trail. Just a 2000 foot high, 70 degree climb, on anything but stable land—with no trail—and I asked, "Do you want to go up this way or stroll inland a bit where a road will take us up and around a much easier way to the overlook?" You looked at that crazy climb and said, "Let's go up here."

When we got to the top, we looked down over that edge that was too fresh, and we realized that forty feet of the edge of the world had just fallen into that ocean just days ago, taking the trail with it. We had started a new trail. You do that with every adventure.

You light up my life. And every room you enter. I am constantly amazed by you, how you have time and care for every person you meet. When our worlds collided a second time, I found a welcoming space of joy and sharing that is your circle of friends and family, and they welcomed me warmly, and you may not know it, but they were also protective of you and your heart. And that is impressive to me. I will keep that, in my heart.

We can not know how the trail ahead might be. But I know it will have much joy, excitement and care of each other at the center of a wonderful circle of trust, love and family. And even if it is a steep climb at times, on the edge of the world with only crashing waves on the fallen rocks below, I want to hike it with you and look over that edge together. I will make sure there are new and ordinary things for you to share your wonderment of. I will support you in your dreams, your life, your desires, your art and your heart. And I will do whatever I can to keep you safe, strong and happy.

Mary Anne

I wondered how best to start this.
I'll begin with: I love you.
Wow, life is interesting —
The twists and turns,
The highs and lows,
The bittersweet and wonderful.
This is a wonderful moment.
Who knew that we would stand here so many years after the first time we met...
Making this commitment.
I am happy and excited to join with you
And our beautiful families and friends gathered here.
Our lives are full and we are rich.
Meeting you when I was 22 was a whirlwind of emotion and fun...
Re-meeting you 25-ish years later was just as refreshing and wonderful.
Many things have been serendipitous for us...
From our mutual friend, Megan in Tucson, inviting us to the same party because she thought we would have fun together — to our chance meeting at Dance Theater West many years later.
I recently found an envelope of letters I wrote to my parents from 1987 when I was in graduate school at U of A (thanks, Mom, for saving

EVERYTHING!). In one letter, I share that I met this guy, Jonathan — that he was creative and fun, talented, and... I really liked him.

An actor and a dancer — may we continue to move through our life with a sense of wonder.

Here we are — the emotional support, daily love, and connection that I feel with you continues to draw me in, bring me comfort, joy, and excitement.

You are someone I can count on, be creative with, share life with, and laugh with.

Your sense of adventure, and humor, your kindness, and your value for/of family — aligns with my values.

Freedom, honoring each other, letting each other be fully who we are — separately and together is an art form that we will strive to hone on this journey.

I am so happy that we make each other's lives better by being together —

I love our creative projects, our outdoor adventures and travels, and our day-to-day lives together.

Knowing the most important people in my life; William and Amanda and my whole family — see how happy we are and embrace you means so much to me and I feel lucky to gain your family as well.

I feel the support and love of our friends — our village — our chosen family.

We are so blessed and I am grateful.

I find it fascinating how we both have "in charge" types of personalities yet we find ways to ebb and flow and agree and support and move through things together.

I appreciate how you authentically celebrate my happy moments and stand by me in the difficult ones.

I love how you laugh at my silliness, and how you can also delve into deep conversations with me.

Two particular conversations come to mind...
When I asked you what you thought the meaning of life was, you confidently said "love."
I had never narrowed it down like that.
It felt like a relief to hear it — it filled my heart,
and it was a step closer to knowing you were the one for me.
Another question I asked you was,
What do you think our biggest commonality is?
And you said, "we both love life."
Again, I felt happiness — a sense of calm and "rightness" when I heard this.
I am glad we have found each other — again. And that we choose to continue to love life — together.

A truly abundant romantic relationship like Mary Anne and Jon's takes that "continuous, committed effort" Zadeh writes about. It also takes faith, trust, and a mutual desire to grow. It is a strong belief of mine that if we are not growing we are dying. It's essential that we surround ourselves with people who are growing and who inspire us to grow. As Mary Baker Eddy wrote, "Growth is the mandate of eternal mind." When you have a partner who encourages you to learn and implement ideas like the one you see in this book, you have a partner for life.

Sharing Your Abundance with the People You Love

One obvious way you can share your abundance with the people you love is to give them the books that made an impact on you. At every wedding I attend, I give a package of my favorite books to build abundant relationships with, including: *Striving Instincts* by Kathy Kolbe, *Clifton Strengthsfinder* by Tom Rath, *The Five Love Lan-*

guages by Gary Chapman, *The Treasure Tree* by John Trent, and *My First 300 Babies* by Gladys Hendricks.

I believe the best marriage and business tool is the Kolbe profile. It's only $55, and this is money well-spent for self-knowledge and investment in your own growth. I cannot fathom working on a project with someone without knowing their Kolbe score. (I immediately looked up Kristen's before approaching her about writing this book together!)

Another book I think is essential for growing in your relationships is *Complaint Free World* by Will Bowen— it is a lifestyle changer. It is an instrumental part of creating culture in companies and families. I wouldn't be who I am without it. I share it with anyone who will give me two minutes to listen. Solving problems, or resolving complaints, does sometimes require money. Sometimes the best way to solve a legitimate complaint is to write a check. Or perhaps you can trade to solve a problem. Sharing your knowledge and resources with others to further their growth and your own is a win-win-win situation.

It is worth calling out one of the books I give away at weddings in particular when it comes to sharing close relationships with people: *The Five Love Languages* by Gary Chapman. I can't imagine raising a kid or dealing with a close relationship where I didn't know their love language. Anybody that's in my vicinity in the home, it's important to know. One of the ways that we have implemented this in our team without actually knowing people's love languages is to ask them, what would they love to have in a benefit—more money or more time off? How we feel valued and appreciated is how we feel loved.

I asked my kids to choose their top two love languages, and within a couple days I could tell from observing them which one was their primary. One of my daughter's love languages is Giving and Receiving Gifts all the way. And even though it's my last love language, I make it a priority. Physical touch is the last of her five and snuggling drives her nuts, so I resist even though it's my top one. I work hard not to pull on her, and instead to give her the love she needs and wants. My sweet son is quality time, and he figured out early on that if he snuggles with mom, he gets more quality time. Love languages can be combined and given to each other in exchange when you know how you each love and like to be loved best.

Ultimately, the way you choose to share your abundance with the people you love is going to be unique to you. What is most important is not how you share it, but that you do. We are here in this human community to help and support each other in our growth. Plus, when we teach someone else what we have learned, we learn it even more and better for ourselves. It also just feels good to give.

Questions for Reflection
- I love the word purpose. What is your family's joint purpose? How does that align with your individual purposes?
- How do you experience abundance in your family?
- What does abundance in a romantic relationship mean to you?
- How do you / would you like to grow with a romantic partner?
- What is your favorite way to share your abundance—of knowledge, resources, time, energy—with the ones you love?

Quick Tips for Sharing the Love and Creating Abundant Relationships

- **Do one small act of kindness for someone you care about today.** Be intentional and do something you know they might not do for themselves or that means a little extra to them.
- **Observe all the ways you see and experience love in your life for a day and write down at least five before bed.** This could be romantic love, familial love, friendship love, animal love, or Divine Love. When we actively acknowledge the love that exists in our lives, we prepare ourselves to create and receive more.
- **Meditate or journal on letting go—of expectations, outcomes, criteria.** When we let go of our predetermined ideas of what should happen in our relationships, we create room for even better opportunities to come in.
- **Tell your partner, child or other loved one what you're most grateful for about them today.** Return to chapter one's concept of proactive gratitude and tell them *before* they demonstrate it. Slow down, look into their eyes, and be present with them when you say it. Really mean it.

BONUS
CHAPTER 9

A Metaphysical Economy

> "Not everything that can be counted counts, and not everything that counts can be counted."
>
> ALBERT EINSTEIN

Our economy began first as a thought. Dr. Matthew Cocks presented as part of Principia College's Lifelong Learning program and addressed this idea: if you put metaphysics on a spectrum on the far right, dualism in the middle and materialism on the left, in Mary Baker Eddy's day (the late 19th and early 20th centuries), dualism was *the* thing. Our society has moved closer to materialism over the last couple centuries. It's been clearly moving back towards dualism lately and onward towards metaphysics over the last twenty years.

Metaphysics is defined by *Merriam-Webster* as "a division of philosophy that is concerned with the fundamental nature of reality and being." The fact that our economy is moving in the direction of metaphysics is promising for shifting our mindset from scarcity towards abundance. The more people value metaphysics, the more humanity will grow.

But what does it mean to value metaphysics and demonstrate it economically? The first person I think of who did this exceptionally well is Joel Weldon, a man I knew in Scottsdale in the 1980s. Joel spent his life as a national speaker before being a speaker was a cool thing. He gave keynotes and was incredibly well-researched. He is my kids' stepgrandfather; his daughter married my kids' dad. He is a classy guy. I remember him saying, "If the economy is in a recession, you can choose not to participate." This is the entire message we want to put forth to encourage prosperity thinkers in this world. *You* are a key part of the *divine* economy, and *you* get to choose the mindset, values, and investments you will bring to the table.

A Spiritual Approach

We're in such an awesome space in our world right now in terms of what's possible. If you want to improve your spiritual life, figure out your relationship with God, Source or Higher Power. We can boldly go forward with God by our side. It can feel weird to approach money from a spiritual perspective since it seems entirely material. However, when our perspective changes and we see it from a spiritual angle, our results change as well.

We work on this perspective shift all the time in my business and my family. There are times I've done a good job, and there are times I've done a deplorable job and ignored it. It is frankly what true financial freedom means—to let go of whatever outcomes show up. If we trust Father Mother God provides us with supply—ideas, relationships, a way forward—even though we may not see it materially at first, we will eventually experience a life of prosperity. Everything begins as ideas.

The Role of Whole Life Insurance

In the 1940s people used to have "savings accounts, whole life insurance, and the home mortgage," according to Steve Utkus, director of the Vanguard Center for Retirement Research, as quoted in the book *Pound Foolish*. Now many people have none of these. The purity of Human Life Value is in danger. Furthermore, Whole Life, the only truly permanent product that wants to be combined with term insurance is being vilified. This is nothing new, we've seen this for the last century, yet it didn't used to be that way.

Due to distorted information coming from the Index Universal Life crowd (or any type of Universal Life, including Fixed and Variable), folks are unclear about the meaning of Permanent and also so focused on Cash Value, they have overlooked the Permanent Death Benefit that Whole Life will ultimately pay.

But don't take my word for it. I want you to know this for yourself. Mary Baker Eddy wrote in *Science and Health with Key to the Scriptures*, "The time for thinkers has come." You'll remember the first Principle of Prosperity is *think*. You care more about your personal finances than anyone else. And while money isn't everything, it affects everything that matters.

Prosperity Thinkers

Prosperity Thinkers fly in the face of established norms, standards and best practices. My husband, Todd Langford of Truth Concepts, and I have created the Prosperity Economics Movement. We work tirelessly to maintain the integrity of our mission and the purity of the message that WL + T = HLV. (It sounds best when you say it out loud.) That is Whole Life + Term Insurance = Human Life Value. This is the standard we bear and the cause we are defending.

Repeatedly I have enjoyed confronting the world's practices

and defying cultural norms. I was provided the opportunity to do so when my parents bought me a dairy cow when I was in the 4th grade. My Grandpa lived on the farm with us and he taught me to milk by hand. This gave our family milk for drinking and cream for making ice cream. You can imagine what responsibility and work ethic this twice daily activity put in my hands.

I endeavored to follow my parents' lead. They taught school five days a week for nine months a year, and every weekend and all summers were dedicated to job #2, our 40-acre farm. Fast-forward to my first year of college, and while I played sports, held a part time job, and was involved in Student Government, I literally felt I had extra time on my hands every single day. So I kept working and learning. To me, those were the two things that created life every day.

Immortal Courage

I like the idea that we can all reflect "immortal courage" and dare to face the world and tell it no. Societal norms, like retirement at age 65, should have no impact on how *you* want to live your life. I want my life to be revolutionary in nature! Besides, my husband has mathematically proven that age 87 is the new 65, once you adjust ages for the amazing longevity we are now experiencing.

Go ahead and upset all that is not upright. Think ideally, live practically. Know that small daily habits are what drive progress, not any one big step. Ignore the views of tradition-bound clergy and the advice of worldly attorneys and politicians. Instead, turn to your Maker for guidance, and establish new standards of practice for yourself and your family. If a spiritual approach isn't for you, consider an inspirational approach. Simply be purposeful in who you follow.

I've made the biggest progress in my life when I narrowed my sources of information. I chose Dan Sullivan of Strategic Coach for business, Christ Jesus and Father Mother God (the name I like for my maker) for spirituality, and Todd Langford for all things financial. Of course I've added some additional mentors throughout my life, and I do believe we can learn something from everyone.

Making Mental Shifts

The best thing about *thinking* is that it can change immediately. When you learn a new approach, your thoughts can switch in an instant. I remember hearing a story from Jordan Adler when he was learning how to fly his helicopter. He said while he had his thumbs on the joy stick, a small shift in his *thought* could help him hit his mark for landing or be over one hundred yards off.

Mental shifts, whether they be followed by moving money, adopting a new habit, or changing our attitudes or behavior, can happen immediately, and they can be impactful immediately. Look to nature for inspiration. Standing outside one day in our garden, there was a pathetic green leaf. The next day, it had transformed into a fully-opened squash blossom. You don't need more discipline, just a new set of habits for change to take place. And it all starts with our thinking, the first Principle of Prosperity.

As we consider the nature of change, it is well to remember that principle is changeless. That is why I've been so grateful to have the 7 Principles of Prosperity to operate from. That solid foundation enables me to test all new ideas as they unfold. And new ideas are important. We cannot keep living in yesteryear.

Your Mission

It is our duty to embrace these new views, and incorporate them into our lives while adhering closely to Principle. Stagnation, whether with our dollars, our minds, or our bodies, is a death sentence. Live your life defined by your mission. And update your mission and your purpose statement constantly. My current version is "shifting thought with a handful of words, in order to create exponential growth."

As we do this, our practice of being human expands and unfolds, it will never stagnate. We are not defined by our jobs, or historical practices. We are defined by our mission. And in order to better fulfill that mission, we must be willing to make real progress. Such progress requires a willingness to change. Now it's important to note that such willingness does not mean that we must throw away all our history. It means that we should simply be willing to do so if that will help us better fulfill our mission.

The divine economy is one in which all of us prosper, and abundance shows up in infinitely creative ways. When we shift our mindset from one of scarcity to one of prosperity, we take our rightful place in this metaphysical economy, and begin to see the fruits of our labor multiply exponentially.

Conclusion

> "It also requires faith that delight will be with you daily, that you needn't hoard it. No scarcity of delight."
>
> ROSS GAY, *THE BOOK OF DELIGHTS: ESSAYS*

Abundance must start in your thought. It's about thinking first and then experiencing it in life. It is imperative that our thinking is at the highest possible level around everything that we're dealing with. Of course, we don't live our lives like that day to day. Sometimes we wake up that way, but more often than not, we don't wake up in an abundance mindset—or we do and something goes haywire in our lives early in the day.

So even more important than *having* an abundance mindset is *gaining* one, fighting for one, creating one in our thinking. There's been numerous times in my life where an unexpected thing happened—relationship, financial, business, legal, home issues—that caused a disconnect. It's not even the question: what are you going to do about it? The first question is what are you going to *think* about it.

As I mentioned before, I grew up in 4-H, showing in the county fairs and state fairs from 4th to 12th grade. It was an integral part of my life. I showed dairy cattle, pigs and sheep. Pigs are very smart; you actually show them with a cane to let them turn left or right, stop or go, based on where you tap the cane on their body. I had won numerous awards, massive ribbons, and trophies throughout junior high and high school.

My senior year, I came into the show ring with my pig, and it was *not* that pig's day. That pig absolutely, positively refused to do anything I tried to get it to do. 4-H is all about showmanship; there are crowds watching and now my pig's not moving! Finally the judge came over and said, "It looks like you're having a bad day; just stay there." I was mortified internally, but I'm in a show ring with an entire crowd. I had been taught by my parents and my life experiences, you've got to get it together or keep it together.

I knew I had to hold it together, which meant right there in that moment I had to get it together physically while mentally, I was falling apart inside. I had to have grown men with boards help me get my pig out of the ring. I don't remember what happened after, but I do remember that I could control my thinking. And that enabled me to get through a sticky situation and be okay with it. If I had let my thinking go then and gotten all worried about the crowds and how it was my last time showing a pig, I would've started crying right there in the ring. It definitely wasn't the right time to do that. The best thing to do was to just stand there and not try to fix it because it wasn't fixable.

Even in the midst of frustration or chaos, your thinking can be controlled. Because of that, you can control your body (like how I did not burst into tears), and then you can control how you are "being" in that space. I love the quote from Ralph Waldo Emerson,

"Your actions speak so loudly, I can not hear what you are saying." Sometimes we see someone who is scared or overconfident that causes them to be a certain way in the space, but their actions are actually overcoming their voice.

You've got to switch your thinking so you can be calm, graceful, and accepting in the face of loss. Though that was clearly an embarrassing moment for me, it was not the end of the world. I could go on and live my life. I still had two other animals to show, and I needed to take care of them. Your thinking controls your being, which controls everything else that's occurring.

Abundance as a word can have such a broad range of meanings, just like the term "value." We can be discussing material, spiritual, inspirational, or emotional value or abundance. So often when we hear the word abundance, we immediately go to material abundance. In this situation, showing the pig, I wasn't going to get material abundance. So what could I get?

In that example, I got what I would call spiritual or inspirational abundance. How I handled the situation and the grace I held allowed me to physically walk out of the ring and not blow up and get mad, or break down and cry (both logical, but both would have only made things worse). In this case, the spiritual and inspirational abundance enabled me to save face in the best way possible, get out of the ring, and deal with what was in front of me for the rest of the day in a community that had supported and watched me for years.

The lesson I gained here gave me something far more valuable than material abundance. In this particular case, the whole fair experience let me release a space in my childhood that had been very important, and prepare to move on to the next space in my life (going early to college to play soccer in a different state). I wasn't going to be able to care for my animals anymore, and I had to get rid of them all. In a way, having these negative things happen created more abundance in the form of time, geography, and mental focus. I was done with that part of my life, and it was a clear "you're done" marker.

Often we don't have the answer to what's next. Asking that question is important when it comes to abundance. We're going to get a lot of abundance in areas we want. But sometimes it's time to move on. I then experienced the next arena of abundance while playing soccer. That ability to shift states—geographical states and states of focus—has proved vital throughout my life. I have transitioned through family situations due to marriages and divorces. I am always seeking an abundance mentality.

Spiritual, inspirational and emotional abundance—when we focus on these first, the material abundance will come. It's so natural for our human brains to go to the scarcity space of material abundance. Nevertheless, it's a reminder when we don't get the material abundance we are seeking to look deeper, further, towards the lessons that teach us what really matters.

In conclusion, I'd like to share a final story of a dear friend of mine, Noah Kelsch. He went through a harrowing health challenge and came out the other side with a renewed sense of what abundance truly means. Here is his story in his own words below:

In August of 2013 I was admitted to the hospital. I was in a bad way and doing all I could to remain conscious. My wife Holly and I knew for some time that my energy levels were low but didn't have answers as to why. After several blood tests it was determined my red blood and platelet levels were critically low. Over the next few days, I received multiple blood transfusions and was told to make an appointment with a blood cancer specialist. After visiting the oncologist and many more tests and some bone marrow biopsies, it was determined I had bone marrow failure and a form of leukemia. This was obviously a massive shock to my wife Holly and I, as well as our 4 children. Up to this point we'd dealt with many challenges in life but this was on a whole other level. I've always had an ingrained determination to accomplish anything I put my mind to, but this was a challenge like none other we'd faced and one that didn't have a very high survival rate. One thing that became crystal clear was that without Divine intervention and a lot of effort on our part, death was the inevitable outcome. Over the next year and a half we spent a lot of time in the cancer center and hospitals, running many tests and multiple bone marrow biopsies and ended up needing over 70 red blood transfusions and as many platelet transfusions. We also spent tens of thousands of dollars and a tremendous amount of time seeking out any alternative, holistic cure that might be out there. Nothing we did seemed to have any effect and my condition continued to deteriorate.

I was blessed to experience angels and guides from the other side, frequently interacting with me as we navigated this journey. I was even given the choice to continue to live on this earth or leave my earthly body and pass on to the other side. Although not privy to what it looked like to continue in this earthly body, ultimately, my choice was to stay. I felt strongly that I had more to learn here on earth in this body and had more to contribute to humanity before crossing over/dying. Through the miracle of Divine guidance, over time I was shown how to heal my spiritual, mental, and emotional bodies. I was blessed with a sneak peek of what's in store for us after we die and was given a completely different perspective of the purpose of life and what's truly important. I was shown that in order to overcome cancer, I had to let go of the notion of fighting it. That is a mind-set of scarcity and has a very low vibrational energy. Also, what we resist will continue to persist. I was shown to completely surrender to the reality of what I was going through and be open to all possibilities.

By late 2014, my physical body had deteriorated to a point that without massive medical intervention I wouldn't have lasted much longer. Blood and platelet transfusions were required almost weekly. It was advised I go in for a bone marrow transplant. Otherwise, the doctors would be forced to send me home to die. Bone marrow transplants are harrowing at best and a death sentence at worst, so this is not a light decision. We were running out of time, having exhausted every other possible remedy we were aware of. Not seeing any other viable option, we set a date for me to be admitted to the hospital for an extended stay while the bone marrow transplant was to take place. Going in, they advised us that for every day I didn't get up out of the hospital bed and move, we could expect an additional three days to the added to the length of time I was in there. With Holly and the kids at home, I was determined to get back to them as soon as possible. Each day I woke up, I would thank my Creator for the gift of life and make an effort to get up and move. Some days this proved very difficult, and I didn't feel like moving at all. The determination to get out of the hospital as quickly as possible drove me to walk the hospital hallways at least 2 to 3 times a day. After being released from the hospital, my dear wife Holly nursed me back to health over the next year. I made a full recovery and am healthier and certainly more happy than I've ever been.

There is an analogy out there that says a hen will peck all day to feed one chick or peck all day to feed ten chicks. When facing death, most daily worries just lose importance. Even worrying about bills, house payments, and food become an afterthought. In letting go of the worry, everything seems to fall into place perfectly and abundance seems to flow naturally. As if hanging on to those worries is what gives them power and relevance. Having the mindset of abundance is key. As if the Universe aligns itself to provide all things once we change our mindset to that of knowing everything will work out for our highest good.

It's certainly not necessary to go through a tragedy or near death expe-

rience in order to have an abundant mindset. Once we let go of the belief that life must be hard or that there isn't enough to go around or that we're not enough, a whole new world is opened up to us and we can be our authentic self and live a life of divine purpose. In doing this, we can truly serve one another and share all of our gifts. One candle can light one million more candles and still not have its light dimmed.

—Noah Kelsch

Though I say goodbye for now, I invite you to explore the tools in the Appendix, as well as the Notes and Recommended Resources. I hope the items you find contribute to your ability to implement some of the ideas you've read—whether you prefer to listen, watch, read, or do—and I look forward to seeing how your newfound prosperity thinking will transform the world.

Appendix 1: Focus Wheel

FOCUS WHEEL INSTRUCTIONS

The 8 sections in the Focus Wheel represent balance.

- Taking the center of the wheel as 0 and the outer edge as 5, rank your **level of satisfaction** with each area out of 5 by drawing a straight or curved line to create a new outer edge (see example).
- The new perimeter of the circle represents **your 'Focus Wheel'**. Is it a bumpy ride?

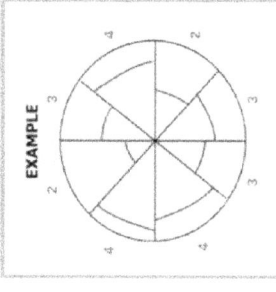

EXAMPLE

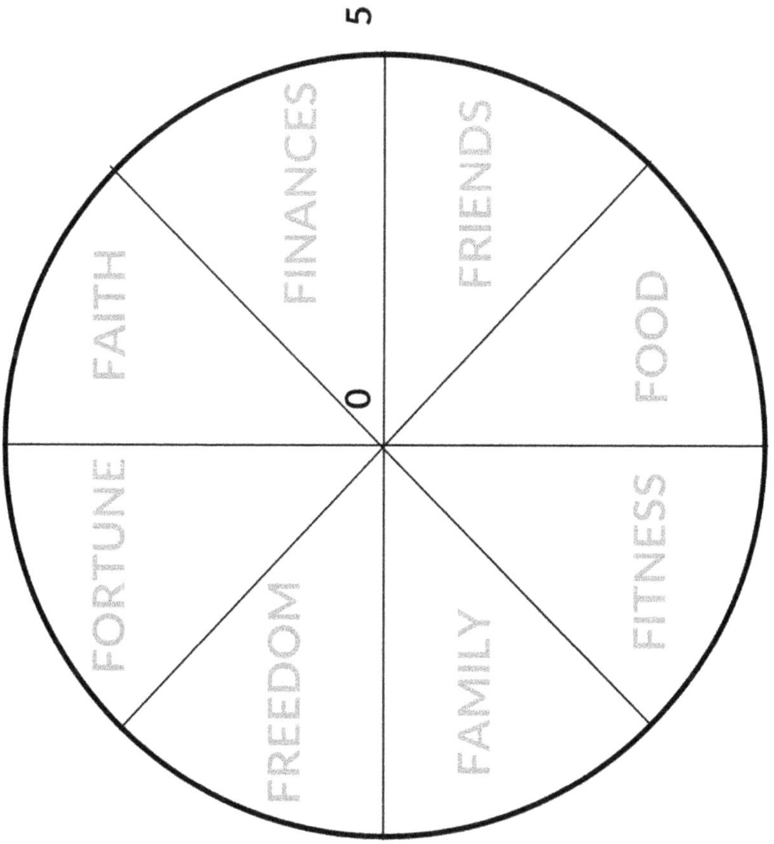

Focus Wheel sections: FAITH, FINANCES, FRIENDS, FOOD, FITNESS, FAMILY, FREEDOM, FORTUNE (center = 0, edge = 5)

Appendix 2: 7 Principles of Prosperity

1. **Think**: Owning a prosperity mind-set eliminates poverty; scarcity thinking keeps you stuck.
2. **See**: Increase your prosperity by adopting a "big picture" perspective in which you can see how each one of your economic decisions affects all the others. Avoid financial "tunnel vision".
3. **Measure**: Always measure your opportunity costs – what your dollars could earn if you did not spend or commit them elsewhere. Awareness of opportunity costs enables you to recover them. Ignore this at your peril.
4. **Flow**: The true measure of prosperity is cash flow. Don't focus on net worth alone.
5. **Control**: Those with the gold make the rules. Stay in control of your money rather than relinquishing control to others.
6. **Move**: The velocity of money is the movement of dollars through assets. Movement accelerates prosperity; accumulation slows it down. Avoid stagnation in assets where dollars accumulate but are not put to use.
7. **Multiply**: Prosperity comes readily when your money "multiplies" – meaning that one dollar does many jobs. Your money is disabled when each dollar performs only one or two jobs.

© 1999 Kim D. H. Butler

Appendix 3: Human Life Value Calculators and Explanation

The Cash Flow Calculator, from Truth Concepts: Human Life Value

This is a transcript from Truth Training, the 3 day event Todd Langford and I teach (typically to financial strategists, though sometimes our clients attend). It has been edited for clarity.

How many of you promote and understand Human Life Value? I think that it's really important. If you sell human life value you probably sell quite a bit of term insurance along with some Whole Life Insurance. Yes, it's going to take term insurance to fill that gap between the Whole Life policy and full Human Life Value. Understand this is a "death benefit" discussion, not a cash value discussion.

I know some of the language that exists on the internet is about how bad the death benefit is and I think it's creating a problem of liability for the advisor. Whether you do a certain strategy or not and it's just about creating money on the side or whatever else, in your clients mind, you are their life insurance professional.

If you do not at least offer human life value, even if clients may not take it, I think you've got some liability issues.

I would offer Human Life Value and we do that a lot. Do we typically find people that can do maximum Paid Up Additions on a whole life policy on full human life value? Not very often, therefore, term insurance is there to fill the gap. Is term insurance good or bad? Yes. Right. BOTH!

Term insurance is just what it is, right, just like anything, it can be used in the wrong strategy and then that's bad. It's not the term insurance that's bad though, it's the strategy. And short term, term insurance is a great tool when used the right way.

So, where does this number on human life value come from? That's a very difficult thing for people to get their head around. We're used to learning from the insurance companies with their rules of thumb that 30 times income for younger people or 10 times income for older people is the number.

There were some actuarial numbers that were used to determine those generalizations that we use to calculate how much somebody could qualify for in death benefit. What I will tell you is the insurance companies are not going to insure you for more than you're worth. There is no such thing as 'making someone rich'.

If the insurance company thinks you're worth that much, then you're worth that much. Okay that is your economic human life value, but it's difficult for somebody who makes $150,000 to see a need for $3 million in death benefit at 20 times earnings right?

They say, "I don't want to leave him or her rich, when I'm gone".

What I will tell you is you cannot leave anybody rich with life insurance, the best you can hope to do is replace their economic human life value, and only if they don't expect any substantial raises along the way.

So all you can get is still going to be less than what it's going to take to replace your income. That makes sense. But if we go back to the question of how can somebody making $150,000 a year imagine $3 million? How can somebody making $250,000 a year imagine leaving $5 million?

What if we are able to see what the cash flow coming off that large lump sum death benefit actually looks like? And then, when put in perspective, we can see why that number makes sense.

All right, so let's look at the Truth Concepts calculator graphic on the opposite page (Fig. A).

We'll take a 35-year-old out 30 years to age 65 so we'll put 30 years in our years to illustrate. I want to find out what their net cash flow is. Then I can see what lump sum would be necessary to put into an account so it would pay out their income. They're making $150,000 gross so the insurance company will allow them as a general rule of thumb, $3 million of death benefit. But let's see **what we actually have to replace in after tax income.**

Figure A

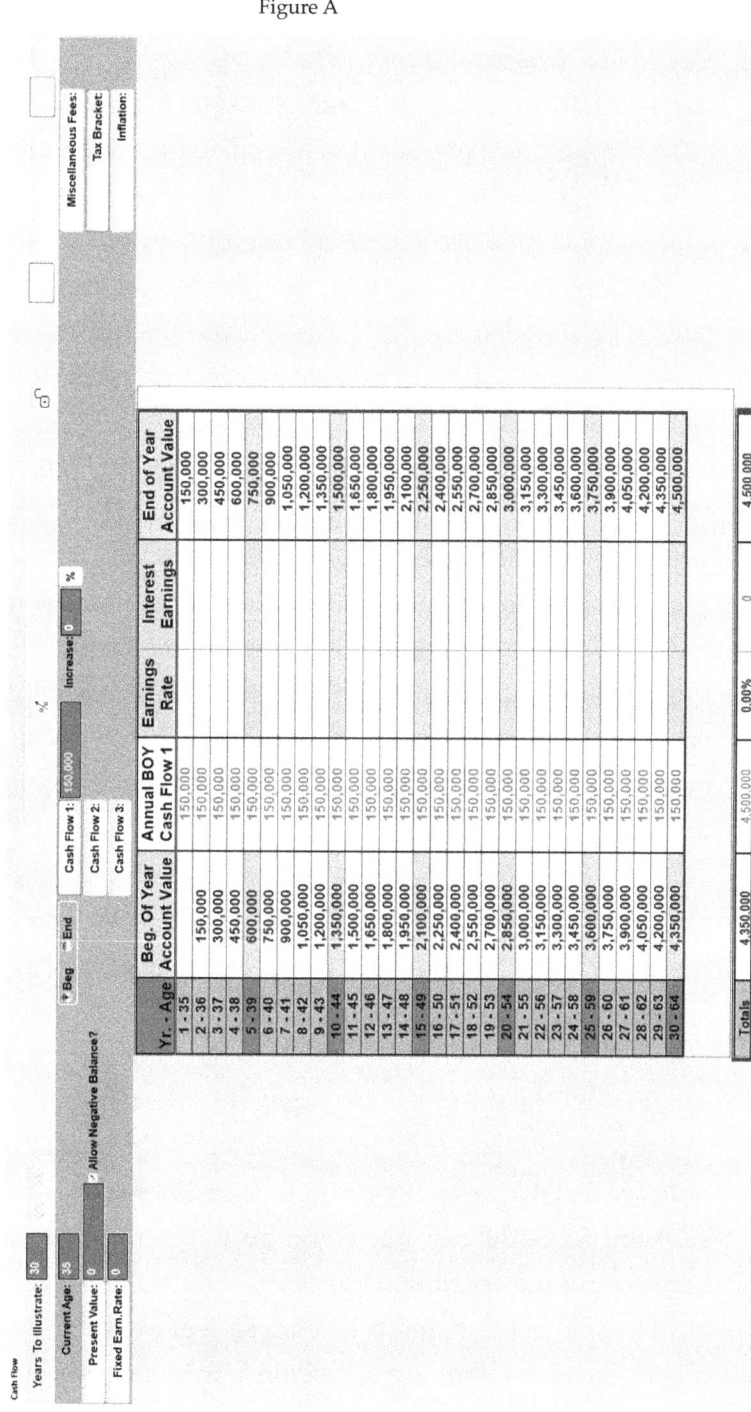

Cash Flow Graphs: Human Life Value

After some tax analysis, **we want $133,000 to appear every year.**

Now, are they going to be happy with a level $133,000 from now on?

No, you know, **we expect at least a 4% cost of living raise.**

So, looking at the Truth Concepts calculator on the opposite page (Fig. B), what we see is this—increasing income (in the highlighted column with the big black border) that we actually want to replace, starting at $133,000 and growing.

Now down here at the bottom of that highlighted column, this is hard to manage mentally at $415,000, but is $415,000 going to buy any more than $133,000 does today?

I would argue it's going to buy less. Why, because more of that income is going to be exposed to those higher tax brackets. So even from a growth standpoint it's the same dollars due to inflation, and we're increasing by four percent after tax, yet, we're going to pay more taxes on those higher incomes. So it's actually going to spend like less but we'll go with that for now.

Now, on the top left is a button that saves us having to go through a whole bunch of calculations on this. **We can click where it says "Present Value."** And it will calculate a number there. This is the net present value of a future stream of increasing income.

And that number is $3,990,000, which represents Human Life Value (Fig. C on the following page). And we can see that we ended up with zero dollars at the end. Since **we could earn money on that side fund at 4%, then it's going to take $3,990,000, so that we can pull out $133,730 and up, going on down the line, and end up zeroing out the account at age 65.**

There is another piece of danger that we have to be careful about. For those that are left behind, it seems like all the money

Figure B

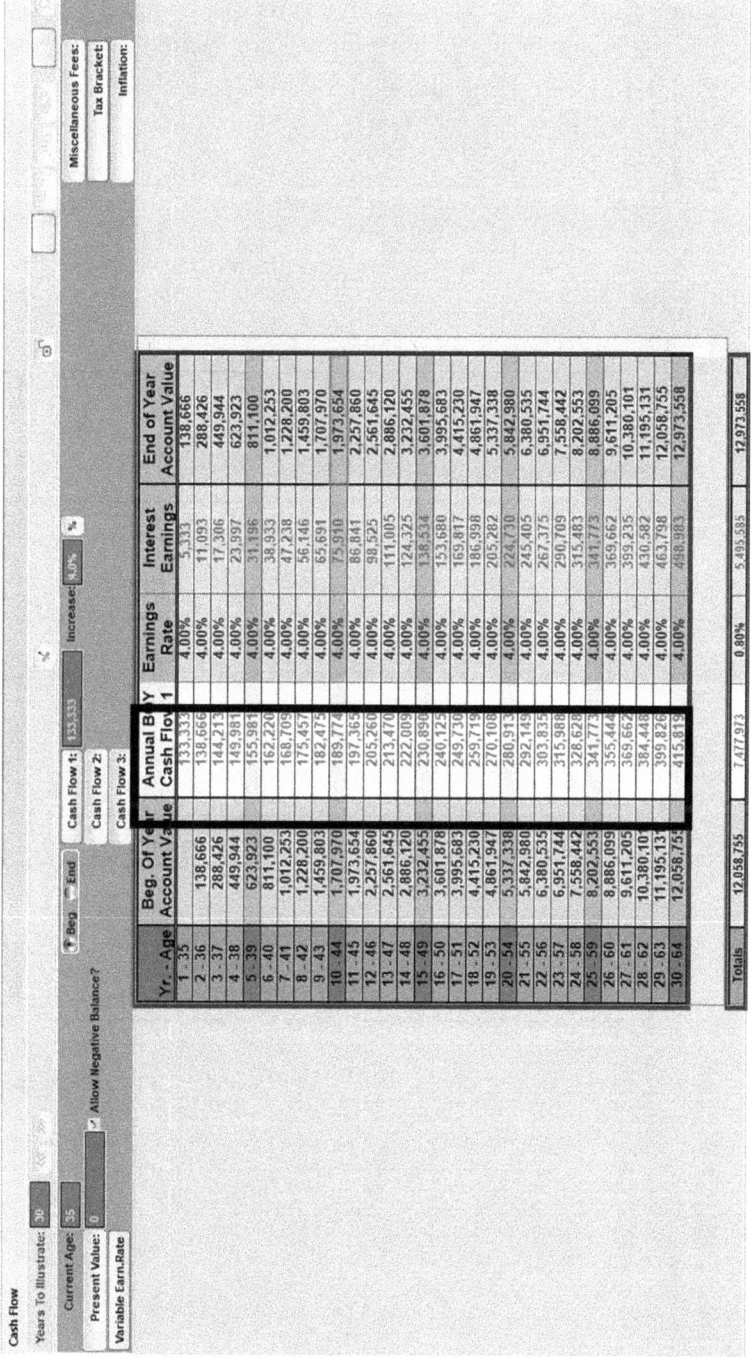

Figure C

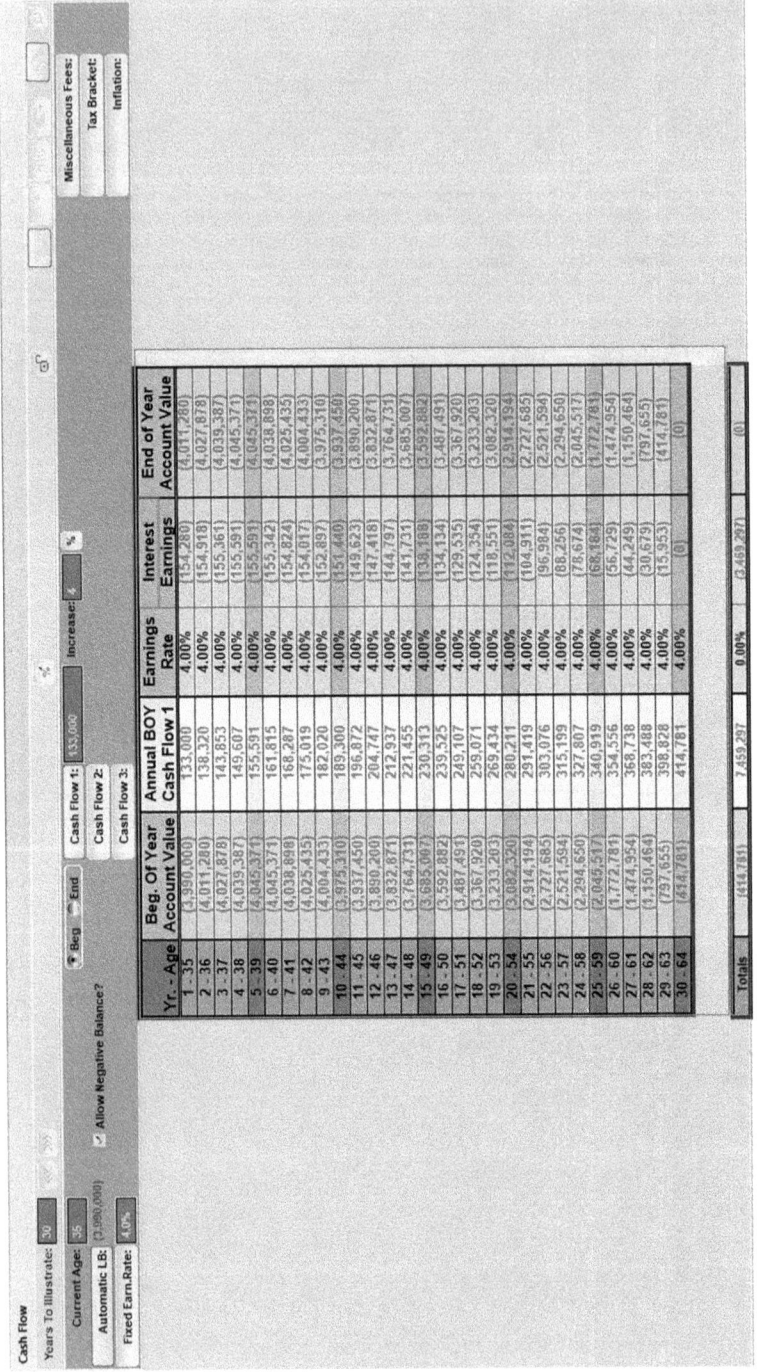

in the world to them. If a premature death occurs, and that money gets blown. Then, they're out of money.

Also, they're out of money at age 65, so that means they should have been saving all along the way, just like they would have been if that individual was living and earning that income. **We're replacing human economic value. It's not a license to spend.**

This is also what's interesting: so many people buy life insurance and forget about it. What happens to a million dollar term policy, over time.. is it less because of inflation? Typically $1/3$ less over 30 years. Look at what happens here.

We started at $3.9 million and we actually see this account has to grow, for a period of time before it actually starts dropping as to what the need is to finish that time frame. That's in order to compensate for that increased cost of living.

So the $3.9 million from the insurance company will not actually fix this problem because it's even less than what's actually needed.

Now I have had success before sending this to the Insurance Company and getting them to issue more than what they were willing to because of the proof.

What I use this for is just for the client to understand the amount of insurance that we're talking about, is going to be less than what it's actually going to take.

Even though it's all we can get from the insurance company. So it's not a crazy amount of money. **It's also important, I think, that the family understands how this works, so that they don't go on a spending spree.** It would be easy to do when you have that much money dumped into your space.

It's a lot easier for people to look back than it is to look forward. When this person sees $415,000 in the future, it is difficult to believe. We can help them by having them look back 10 years and think about the income they earned then, compared to now.

Sometimes charts are easier. This one on the opposite page (Fig. D) looks at just what the values are. So we started with $3.9 million dollars and we ended up with zero.

If you want help with your own Human Life Value, reach out to Kim or any financial strategist who uses TruthConcepts.com calculators. There are a few other calculators in the marketplace that use Human Life Value, yet most only use "needs analysis". We aren't a fan of those because all insurance is purchased to replace the full value of something, not only what is needed. If you drive a $50,000 car, you insure it for $50,000, not $30,000 because that is only what you "need".

Figure D

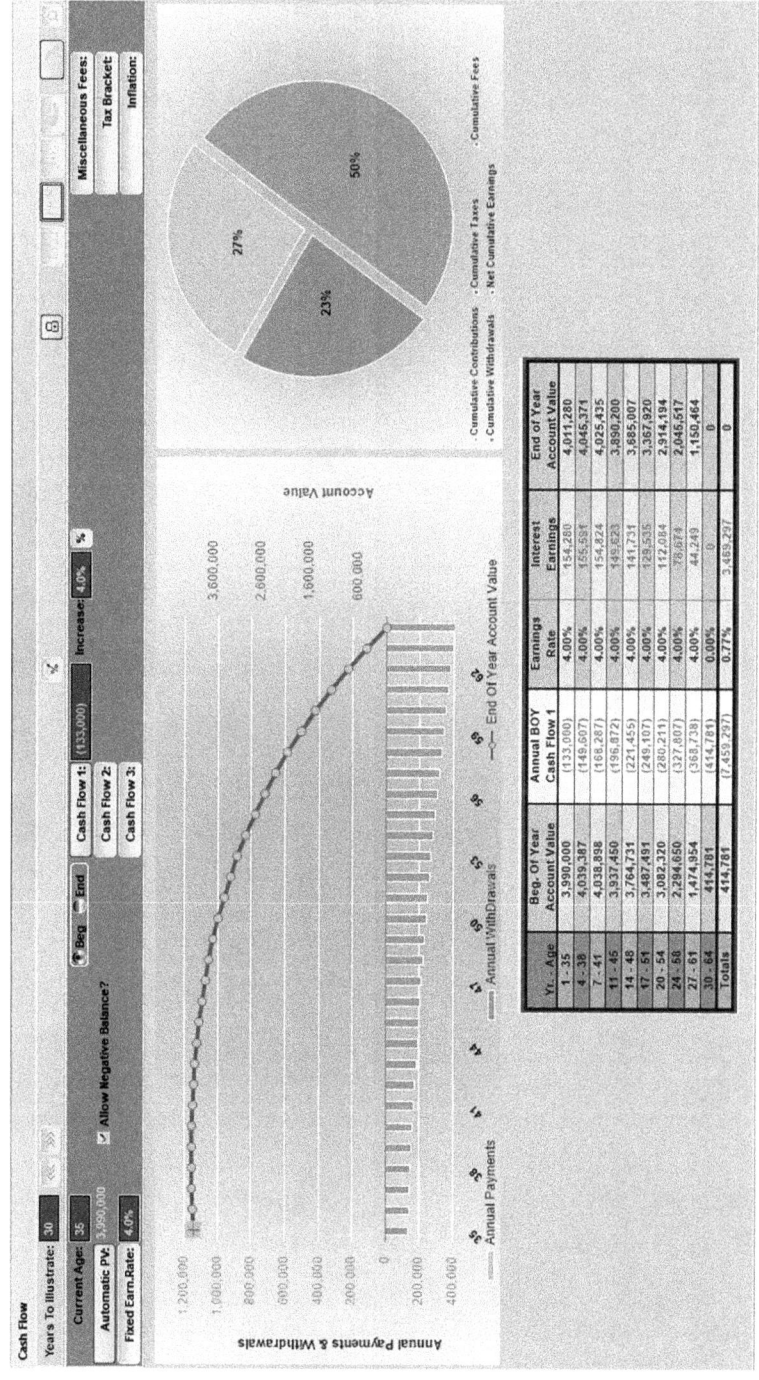

Acknowledgments

I want to acknowledge a long list of people in my life who help me do the mental work. In each case I've tried to list the specific thing they do, so that you (the reader) can find people in your life to help you in the way this group helps me! In no particular order, they are:

Todd Langford, my husband of TruthConcepts.com fame, who exemplifies Prosperous Thinking with me every single day in our "house of both!"

Tammi Brannan, my sister of BlueprintProcess.com fame, who helps me Bust Scarcity Lies almost every single day.

George Huang, my dear friend and mentor, who contributed such meaningful stories and wisdom for this book.

Nancy McVeigh, virtual workout buddy and positive thinker extraordinaire! I am always grateful for our 2 hours a week that we "zoom" together, as well as daily "50 pushups" texts.

Dan Sullivan & Babs Smith, founders of Strategic Coach, mentors for over 30 years, my go-to source for entrepreneurial thought leadership.

Theresa Sheridan, long standing Prosperity Thinkers' team member who is my "right arm" in all things PT, as a "brain on" contributor, positive focus leader, and life insurance expert.

Rae Ann Vitense, Kolbe 7626 team member who loves all our clients as much as I do and shows them every day with an amazing dedication to creating a positive environment.

Elizabeth Hagenlocher, the writer for all things Kim and Todd who has adopted our mindsets, language, thought patterns, values, and care for quality with high standards & enthusiasm.

Debbi Sherman, technological wizard, great marketing mind, and very hard worker who has embraced both teams' work with gusto, a "give first" attitude, and willingness to figure things out.

Cole Brannan, video expert and social media point person, who has gained traction and capabilities daily in a very fast-moving environment, while digging deep for abundant thinking.

Spencer Shaw, Prosperity Podcast co-host, who brings us all fabulous and fun research on subjects to speak about, while also producing and helping me be a guest on others' podcasts.

Katie Fitzgerald, TC community builder, force for good with all things pointed to Prosperity Thinking and armed with tools to bust (with flair!) any scarcity mindsets that pop up.

Carrie Putman, of BookkeepingHelpers.com fame, who has taken the Prosperity Perspective to a higher level every one of the 30+ years we've worked together—here's to 30 more!

Dan Hays, purchaser of the famed milk cow when I was in 4th grade, believer that all good things come to those who work on farms, and still serving student teachers in his mid 80s.

Gabe Mendoza, also a 30-year + teammate, technical and human all at the same time, full of positivity, a "can-do" attitude, savior of lost google docs, and instrumental in our smart home.

Andrew Chapman, who has helped us with books from Day 1 and is always willing to be an example of prosperous work inside his SocialMotionPublishing.com arena.

Kristen Hugins, co-author and strong Prosperity Thinker herself, always bringing a smile to our meetings from her home at Joyfull Communications, demonstrating that a smile gives first.

—Kim Butler

First of all, I'm deeply grateful to Kim Butler for the opportunity to co-author this book; working with her has truly been life-changing.

Thank you to my children, Kyler and Inara, for your infinite patience and support. Thank you to my immediate family, Debbie Morand, David Olsen, and Kimberly Olsen for brainstorming, bouncing ideas around, and cheering me on. And thank you to my friends: Lexi Henderson, Alicia Yaeger-Booth, Mary Barcena, and Steve Creighton, for supporting me throughout the process in your own unique, abundant ways.

I could not have done all of this without my coach and dear friend, Michael Goodman. And I am thankful beyond words to my mentor, Carolyn Bond, for helping me become both a better writer and editor with each book I work on.

Deep gratitude goes to my dear friends, Mary Anne Herding and Jon Mincks, for sharing your love story and vows so freely. May we each experience a love like yours at least once in a lifetime.

I would also like to thank each of the authors we quoted or referenced whose abundant ideas inspired us and added depth and meaning to this book.

And lastly, I am grateful for you, dear reader, for giving us a reason to write this book, as well as the hope that one day, through learning and collaboration, we all may live abundant lives full of prosperity.

—Kristen Hugins

About the Authors

Kim D. H. Butler is helping Americans build wealth... WITHOUT Wall Street risks! Kim is president of Prosperity Thinkers, a personal finance firm that serves clients in all 50 states. Along with her husband Todd Langford of Truth Concepts financial software, Kim is also the co-founder of Prosperity Economics Movement.

A recognized expert on whole life insurance and financial strategies. Kim has authored paradigm-shifting books such as: Live Your Life Insurance, Busting the Life Insurance Lies, and Perpetual Wealth.

Driven to find a better way, Kim studied the commonalities between wealth builders. She observed what worked and didn't work in the real world, and found synergy between certain strategies and principles. These common principles later became the "7 Principles of Prosperity" of the Prosperity Economics Movement.

In 1999, Kim dedicated herself to the principles of Prosperity

Economics. Her work as a Prosperity Economics Advisor has been recommended by financial thought leaders and authors such as Robert Kiyosaki (Rich Dad, Poor Dad), Tom Dyson, publisher of the Palm Beach Letter investment newsletter, Tom Wheelright (Tax Free Wealth), and Garrett Gunderson (Killing Sacred Cows). She has been interviewed by Robert Kiyosaki, consulted with the Palm Beach Letter, and featured on many popular podcasts, including her own — The Prosperity Podcast on iTunes.

As the owner of Joyfull Communications, **Kristen Hugins** ghostwrites, co-writes, and edits books and other content for businesses and individuals who have compelling stories to tell that drive action and meaningful impact. She believes that words are powerful. When we use them wisely, we can transform each other—and the world.

With over 20 years of experience writing and creating content for businesses and organizations, it is her purpose to express joy through communication in order to help others share their gifts with the world.

Notes

Introduction

Wayne W. Dyer, *Change Your Thoughts, Change Your Life: Living the Wisdom of the Tao* (Carlsbad, CA: Hay House, 2007).

"How Your Thinking Creates Your Reality," *Psychology Today*, accessed February 4, 2025, https://www.psychologytoday.com/us/articles/how-your-thinking-creates-your-reality.

The Holy Bible, New King James Version, Hebrews 11:1.

Chapter 1: Proactive Gratitude

"Holy Joy," *Christian Science Sentinel*, accessed February 4, 2025, https://sentinel.christianscience.com/shared/view/2obiuyxzk5i?s=e.

Ken Honda, *Happy Money: The Japanese Art of Making Peace With Your Money* (New York: Simon & Schuster, 2019).

Ellen Grace O'Brian, *The Jewel of Abundance: Finding Prosperity through the Ancient Wisdom of Yoga* (Novato, CA: New World Library, 2018).

"Understanding the Brain Science Behind Giving and Receiving Gifts," *University of Arizona News*, accessed February 4, 2025, https://news.arizona.edu/story/understanding-brain-science-behind-giving-and-receiving-gifts#:~:text=A%3A%20There%20is%20a%20decent,associated%20with%20reward%20and%20pleasure.

Chapter 2: Learn to Use and See Money as a Tool

"Wealth Dynamics Quiz," accessed February 4, 2025, https://wealthdynamics.geniusu.com/.

Paulo Coelho, *The Alchemist* (San Francisco: HarperOne, 1993).

"Propellers: How Things Fly," *National Air and Space Museum*, accessed February 4, 2025, https://howthingsfly.si.edu/propellers.

Chapter 3: Create—In a Be, then Do Way

"Your Brain on Meditation," *Mindful*, accessed February 4, 2025, https://www.mindful.org/your-brain-on-meditation/.

Chuck Swindoll, "Doing vs. Being," *Insight for Today*, accessed February 4, 2025, https://www.insight.org/resources/daily-devotional/doing-vs-being.

Chapter 4: Make It Personal: Match Money to Values

James Clear, *Atomic Habits: An Easy & Proven Way to Build Good Habits & Break Bad Ones* (New York: Avery, 2018).

Marie McNamara and John Veeken, *The Values Cards* (Australia: Innovative Resources, 2011).

Kim Butler, *Family Legacy* (Phoenix, AZ: Partners for Prosperity, 2018).

Avery Alder, *The Quiet Year* (Self-published, 2013).

BJ Fogg, *Tiny Habits: The Small Changes That Change Everything* (Boston: Houghton Mifflin Harcourt, 2019).

"Human Life Value Calculator," *Life Happens*, accessed February 4, 2025, https://lifehappens.org/human-life-value-calculator/.

Chapter 5: Intentional Income Design

"16 Remote Jobs That Pay at Least $40 Per Hour," *Yahoo Finance*, accessed February 4, 2025, https://www.yahoo.com/finance/.

Kolbe Profile, accessed February 4, 2025, https://www.kolbe.com/.

Chapter 6: Invest in Your Growth

Dan Sullivan and Benjamin Hardy, *The Gap and the Gain: The High Achievers' Guide to Happiness, Confidence, and Success* (New York: Hay House, 2021).

Kolbe Profile, accessed February 4, 2025, https://www.kolbe.com/.

"How to Fascinate Quiz," accessed February 4, 2025, https://www.howtofascinate.com/.

BluePrintProcess.com, accessed February 4, 2025, https://www.blueprintprocess.com/.

Po Bronson, *What Should I Do with My Life? The True Story of People Who Answered the Ultimate Question* (New York: Random House, 2002).

Stephen Cope, *The Great Work of Your Life: A Guide for the Journey to Your True Calling* (New York: Bantam, 2012).

"CliftonStrengths Assessment," *Gallup*, accessed February 4, 2025, https://www.gallup.com/cliftonstrengths/.

Chapter 7: Collaborate for Exponential Increase

Peter Diamandis, "9 Secrets of Blue Zones: How Many Do You Follow?" accessed February 4, 2025, https://www.diamandis.com/.

Matt Ridley, *The Rational Optimist: How Prosperity Evolves* (New York: Harper, 2010).

Peter Diamandis and Steven Kotler, *Abundance: The Future Is Better Than You Think* (New York: Free Press, 2012).

McKinsey & Company, "How Corporates and Start-ups Can Collaborate Successfully," accessed February 4, 2025, https://www.mckinsey.com/.

The Holy Bible, New International Version, Romans 8:28.

"Why Collaboration Is Critical in Uncertain Times," *Harvard Business Review*, accessed February 4, 2025, https://hbr.org/.

Twyla Tharp, *The Collaborative Habit: Life Lessons for Working Together* (New York: Simon & Schuster, 2009).

General Stanley McChrystal, *Team of Teams: New Rules of Engagement for a Complex World* (New York: Portfolio, 2015).

Brené Brown, *Dare to Lead: Brave Work. Tough Conversations. Whole Hearts.* (New York: Random House, 2018).

"The Power of Proximity: Co-Locating Childcare and Eldercare Programs," accessed February 4, 2025, https://ssir.org/articles/entry/the_power_of_proximity_co_locating_childcare_and_eldercare_programs.

BONUS Chapter 8: Share the Love: Abundant Relationships and Families

Henri Lipmanowicz and Keith McCandless, *The Surprising Power of Liberating Structures: Simple Rules to Release a Culture of Innovation* (Seattle: Liberating Structures Press, 2014).

Prosperity Parents, accessed February 4, 2025, https://prosperityparents.com/.

Armin A. Zadeh, *The Forgotten Art of Love: What Love Means and Why It Matters* (Oakland, CA: Berrett-Koehler, 2017).

Mary Baker Eddy, *Science and Health with Key to the Scriptures* (Boston: The Christian Science Publishing Society, 1875).

BONUS Chapter 9: A Metaphysical Economy

Steve Utkus, as quoted in Helaine Olen, *Pound Foolish: Exposing the Dark Side of the Personal Finance Industry* (New York: Portfolio, 2012).

Recommended Resources

Click on the QR code at the end of this section (page 173) to get a PDF with live links for each of the Recommended Resources you see here. Happy reading, watching, listening, and learning!

KIM'S BOOK SERIES
Here is a suggested order for reading:
   Your Guide to Activating Prosperity (only available at ProsperityThinkers.com, it's Kim's story)
   Busting the Financial Planning Lies (the first book written, a story about two options with your finances)
   Live Your Life Insurance (short primer on using Whole Life as your emergency/opportunity fund)
   Optional: **Busting the Life Insurance Lies** (deeper dive into how Whole Life works; also has a story)
   Busting the Budgeting Lies (why spending plans don't work and what to do instead)
   Busting the Retirement Lies (about 401k plans and options beyond retirement)

Busting the Interest Rate Lies (about mortgages and car loans, a young person's story)

Busting the Real Estate Investing Lies (about the importance of cash flow)

Perpetual Wealth (speaks about legacy beyond money and tells a story about three generations)

Busting the College Planning Lies (helpful for both parents and students)

19 Videos on Values by Kim on YouTube

INSPIRATION

The Message: The Bible in Contemporary Language by *Eugene H. Peterson*

Science and Health with Key to the Scriptures by *Mary Baker Eddy*

The Butterfly Effect: How Your Life Matters by *Andy Andrews*

Abundance: The Future Is Better Than You Think by *Peter Diamandis and Steven Kotler*

A New Earth: Awakening to Your Life's Purpose by *Eckhart Tolle*

The Gap and The Gain: The High Achievers' Guide to Happiness, Confidence, and Success by *Dan Sullivan with Dr. Benjamin Hardy*

The Prosperity Paradigm by *Steve D'Annunzio*

Good People: Stories From the Best of Humanity (*via Upworthy*) by *Gabriel Reilich and Lucia Knell*

The Path to Wealth: Seven Spiritual Steps to Financial Abundance by *May McCarthy*

MONEY

The Mystery of Capital: Why Capitalism Triumphs in the West and Fails Everywhere Else *by Hernando de Soto*

Millionaire Women Next Door: The Many Journeys of Successful American Businesswomen *by Thomas J. Stanley*

The Richest Man in Babylon *by George S. Clason*

The Moral Case for Fossil Fuels *by Alex Epstein*

Myths, Lies, and Downright Stupidity: Get Out the Shovel—Why Everything You Know Is Wrong *by John Stossel*

Tax-Free Wealth: How to Build Massive Wealth by Permanently Lowering Your Taxes *by Tom Wheelwright*

Principles of Economics *by Saifedean Ammous*

Pound Foolish: Exposing the Dark Side of the Personal Finance Industry *by Helaine Olen*

RELATIONSHIPS

Making Love Last Forever *by Gary Smalley*

50 Ways to Create Great Relationships: How to Stop Taking and Start Giving *by Steve Chandler*

The 21 Irrefutable Laws of Leadership: Follow Them and People Will Follow You *by John C. Maxwell*

Striving Zones: How People Act When Free to Be Themselves *by Kathy Kolbe*

StrengthsFinder 2.0 *(via Gallup) by Tom Rath*

The 5 Love Languages: How to Express Heartfelt Commitment to Your Mate *by Gary Chapman*

The Go-Giver Marriage: A Little Story About the 5 Secrets to Lasting Love *by John David Mann and Ana Gabriel Mann*

GROWTH

The Laws of Lifetime Growth: Always Make Your Future Bigger Than Your Past *by Dan Sullivan and Catherine Nomura*

To Sell Is Human: The Surprising Truth About Moving Others *by Daniel H. Pink*

Mindset: The New Psychology of Success *by Carol Dweck*

Side Hustle Bible *by James Altucher*

Rise of the Reader: Strategies for Mastering Your Reading Habits and Applying What You Learn *by Nick Hutchison*

Eleven Rings: The Soul of Success *by Phil Jackson and Hugh Delehanty*

The Education of Millionaires: Everything You Don't Learn in College About How to Be Successful *by Michael Ellsberg*

Clay Water Brick: Finding Inspiration From Entrepreneurs Who Do the Most With the Least *by Jessica Jackley*

Love Works: Seven Timeless Principles for Effective Leaders *by Joel Manby*

Happy Stories!: Real-Life Inspirational Stories from Around the World That Will Raise Your Happiness Level *by Will Bowen*

KIDS

Good Night Stories for Rebel Girls: 100 Tales of Extraordinary Women *by Elena Favilli and Francesca Cavallo*

All of the Tuttle Twins material *by Connor Boyack:*
- Tuttle Twins 12-Book Combo Pack
- The Tuttle Twins Learn About the Law
- The Tuttle Twins and the Road to Surfdom

Who Moved My Cheese: An Amazing Way to Deal With Change in Your Work and in Your Life *by Spencer Johnson*

How Nearly Everything Was Invented *by the Brainwaves (by Jilly MacLeod)*

Secret of the Peaceful Warrior *by Dan Millman*
What Do You Do With a Chance? *by Kobi Yamada*
What Do You Do With an Idea? *by Kobi Yamada*
What Do You Do With a Problem? *by Kobi Yamada*
The Treasure Tree: Helping Kids Understand Their Personality *by John & Cindy Trent and Gary & Norma Smalley*
Value Creation Kid: The Healthy Struggles Your Children Need to Succeed *by Scott Donnell and Lee Benson*
Raising Self-Reliant Children in a Self-Indulgent World: Seven Building Blocks for Developing Capable Young People *by H. Stephen Glenn and Jane Nelsen*

LONGEVITY

Finishing Well: The Adventure of Life Beyond Halftime *by Bob Buford*
Life Force: How New Breakthroughs in Precision Medicine Can Transform the Quality of Your Life and Those You Love *by Tony Robbins, Peter H. Diamandis, and Robert J Hariri*
Untethered Aging *by William Keiper*
If Your Life Were a Business, Would You Invest in It?: The 13-Step Program for Managing Your Life Like the Best CEOs Manage Their Companies *by John Eckblad and David Kiel*
Letters to a Great Grandson: A Message of Love, Advice, and Hopes for the Future *by Hugh Downs*
Click Here When I Die: Making Things Easier for Those You Love *by Jonathan S. Braddock*
Disrupt Aging: A Bold New Path to Living Your Best Life at Every Age *by Jo Ann Jenkins*

FREE DAY BOOKS

The Man Who Listens to Horses: The Story of a Real-Life Horse Whisperer by Monty Roberts

The Rational Optimist: How Prosperity Evolves by Matt Ridley

Fighting Fire by Caroline Paul

The Island of Sea Women: A Novel by Lisa See

Shadow Divers: The True Adventure of Two Americans Who Risked Everything to Solve One of the Last Mysteries of World War II by Robert Kurson

The Only Woman in the Room: A Novel by Marie Benedict

Yes, And: How Improvisation Reverses "No, But" Thinking and Improves Creativity and Collaboration—Lessons from The Second City by Kelly Leonard and Tom Yorton

MOVIES

Last of the Mohicans

Endurance

The Upside

The Rookie

The Woman of the Sea

Invincible *(starring Mark Wahlberg)*

The Miracle Season *(with Helen Hunt)*

The Hundred-Foot Journey

The Best Exotic Marigold Hotel

SONGS

First by Lauren Daigle

Rescue by Lauren Daigle

Keep Your Mind Wide Open by AnnaSophia Robb (star of **Bridge to Terabithia**)

We Didn't Start the Fire *by Billy Joel*
I'm on Fire *by Bruce Springsteen*
Country Strong *(soundtrack)*
Man! I Feel Like a Woman! *by Shania Twain*

Click on the QR code below to get a PDF with live links for each of the resources in this section. Again, we wish you happy reading, watching, listening, and learning!

www.ingramcontent.com/pod-product-compliance
Lightning Source LLC
Chambersburg PA
CBHW070447050426
42451CB00015B/3376